THE BUS TO SHEBOYGAN

An Adult Peek Between the Covers of the Bible

Lori J. Brashear

©Copyright applied for 2006 by L. Brashear

All rights in this book are reserved world-wide

No part of the book may be reproduced in any manner whatsoever without the written permission of the author except brief quotations embodied in critical articles or reviews

For information on reordering please contact:

Vision Publishing
1115 D Street
Ramona, CA 92065
www.visionpublishingservices.com
(760) 789-4700

ISBN # 1-931178-34-8

TABLE OF CONTENTS

Introduction 9
Ch 1 The Itinerary is Always Right (A Parable) .. 11
Ch 2 In The Beginning – Who? 23
Ch 3 Creation? Good Grief, Haven't You Heard About Evolution? 37
Ch 4 In Six Days ? You've Got To Be Kidding 55
Ch 5 That's M' Boy (A Parable) 63
Ch 6 God Loves A Wedding 73
Ch 7 The Problem (It Surely Must Be God's Fault) 81
Ch 8 Sentence Is Passed 103
Ch 9 The Solution (The Gift, A Parable) 113
Ch 10 In The Image Of Adam 125
Ch 11 The Appointment 133
Ch 12 Help! I Think I'm In The Wrong Church . 141
Suggested Readings On Apologetics 151
Bibliography 153

I would like to dedicate this study to all of the pastors who are as concerned as I am regarding the Biblical illiteracy among both the churched and the unchurched and who would like to do something about it.

I would also like to include my husband, whose patience and cooking skills took a turn for the better during the preparation of the study; and George and Lupe Martin whose expertise put the final touches on the book. These three were also my cheering section.

PREFACE

Today we live in a world that is being manipulated by groups of power hungry men. They have their fingers in every pot in the world; politics, banking, education, and even religion. Do you believe your vote counts at the poles? Maybe. Maybe not. Maybe your man of the hour sitting in the President's seat may have already been chosen by others before any vote was taken. Although it is worse today than it has been in past times, power hungry men have always desired to rule the world and make slaves of the people so they, the powerful, can live as potentates. But God has a plan and that plan is for you personally, if you so desire. However, in order to know and understand that plan and apprehend it for yourself, you must know what is within the covers of the Bible.

In trying to talk to many people about the Bible over the past forty years, it has been my sorrow that few have any idea what is going on between its covers. In addition to this it appears that few churches are teaching the Bible today nor have they for years. In that it is my belief that a knowledge of the Bible is necessary for a knowledge of God and being allowed into His Heaven; it has been my desire to write a short and simple study to introduce the Scriptures to the unchurched, or even the churched if they desire, in order that God does not soon close the doors and call in the Great Tribulation period upon them.

This study contains an integrated study of the first four chapters of the book of Genesis with the first four chapters of the book of John. These eight chapters appear to contain an understanding of the core of the Christian faith, why the world is the way it is, what is coming in the future, and can be used to encourage those who have a desire to follow God. It may also lead to the further practice of Bible reading for those God followers who are serious about having a walk with Him.

May this begin many exciting days of listening to God through His word and understanding what He has planned for you.

THE BUS TO SHEBOYGAN
(An Adult Peek between the Covers of the Bible)

INTRODUCTION:

To lay a foundation for your pleasure it has been chosen to present to you here only the first four chapters of two of the books of the Bible, namely, from the Old Testament, Genesis, chapters 1 through 4, side by side with the Gospel (good news) of John, chapters 1 through 4 of the New Testament. This has been chosen, because there is a correlation between these two books and for a short study they give the most cogent information of why the world is in the shape it is in; what Christianity is all about; and why Christ had to die on the cross for us.

Genesis one and John one speak of God, Jesus (who He is), and what they have done. Genesis two and John two speak of a wedding. Genesis three speaks of the problem with the world today and John 3 speaks of the solution to that problem. Both Genesis four and John four speak of the human condition then and now.

Genesis has been known for something over 3,500 years, to have been written by Moses from the mouth of God and the book of John was written by the disciple John, (one of the twelve, not John the Baptist), also from the mouth of God, about the year 85 to 95 A.D.(In the year of our Lord). It is said that the book of John was written in Ephesus (a city in Turkey that is no longer populated), the city that John finally migrated to after his imprisonment on the Greek Isle of Patmos and after the destruction of Israel and the Jewish temple by the Roman, Titus, in 70 A.D.

After chapter four, the books move on in their own direction and Genesis is basically about the beginnings of civilization and the dealings of God with man in the early days of the earth and in the early days of the people of Israel; and John moves on after chapter four and is the story of the doings of Jesus and the reason that the Gospel is called the "Good News".

A Bible reference will be given to you at the beginning of each section and we will only discuss certain points from each chapter. However, it would be good to read the first four chapters of both Genesis and John at one sitting [1]. Then it is always better to read the Bible passage pertaining to each study before starting the study.

May God be with you in this study and it is always appropriate and helpful to pray a little prayer for understanding before reading any of the books of the Bible. God is so excited that you want to read His word that He is about to give a party for you in Heaven, if you like His book [2], that is.

---

[1] All Scripture references are from the New King James Version of the Bible.
[2] See Luke 15:10.

CHAPTER 1

THE ITINERARY IS ALWAYS RIGHT

(a parable):

One day Joe had a mind to go to Sheboygan, so he went down to the bus station to catch the bus to Sheboygan; but lo and behold when he got there, there were hundreds of buses. As he went from bus to bus to find the one labeled "Sheboygan", he found that all the labels on the buses had been covered up. As he stumbled around asking first this one then that where he might find the bus to Sheboygan, he received so many different answers and became so confused that he finally decided to just get on any bus and see where it would take him (after all, weren't all buses alike?). Needless to say, after many days Joe finally ended up in Pasadena and sadder yet, he had spent all of his substance and there was no way back to Sheboygan.

Jerry, on the other hand, was a bit more intelligent about the matter. He first went into the bus station and got an itinerary. He sat down and carefully read and digested it. Then he went to several ticket windows until he found a ticket agent that agreed with the printed itinerary; got instructions as to where the bus was located; got the name of the bus driver; and then he bought a ticket. Using a bit of detective work, he sought out the path to the correct bus all the while asking each bus driver his name. When he found the right bus, Jerry got on the bus. Jerry got to Sheboygan: Joe did not.

What was Joe's problem? He was just too lazy to read and digest the itinerary. However, there was another problem and that was the ticket agents. Most of them, sorry to say, were also giving out the wrong information. Some would pick out a line on the itinerary and continue repeating it until he put you to sleep. Then some would tell you that the itinerary is incorrect and that you must follow his instructions and only pay attention to this line and that line. Then there are those agents who would tell you that the itinerary is totally incorrect and needs to be trashed and he will give you the correct information until the "new itinerary" comes out.

The secret? Don't ever trust the ticket agent. Remember three things and three things only; one, *THE ITINERARY IS ALWAYS RIGHT;* two, there will be no "new itinerary"; and three, the ticket agent who agrees with the itinerary is the only one safe to listen to.

As you must have guessed by now, Sheboygan represents Heaven, the itinerary is the Bible, the ticket agent is the preacher, and the bus driver's name is Jesus; which it is imperative to know in order to get on the right bus. Remember, Jerry made it to Sheboygan, because he read the itinerary before listening to the ticket agent (which includes this writer), or beginning his search for the right bus.

It is a sad commentary on society today that although many people are curious about what is in the Bible, those who teach it must waste precious time proving first, that there is a God; second, who Jesus is; and third proving the credibility of the Bible. God didn't have to do that. In reading the Bible we find that God never tries to prove He exists, He merely takes for granted that we have enough sense to know that. Only in these last two or three generations must we try to prove that which should be obvious to all. However, we must take the world as we find it.

Before proceeding, a good question to ask is how do we know the itinerary (the Bible) is always right? This is most important, because it tells us about God, Jesus, and the Holy Spirit; who they are; what God has done and will do; and most importantly, what it all means to you personally. One warning: Never cut and paste parts of the itinerary (the Bible) you want to believe and do away with parts you don't want to believe. If one part of it is wrong, then the rest can't be trusted either. The Bible is an all or nothing book.

Proving the Bible is a part of a subject called apologetics. By the way, apologetics does not mean we apologize for being Christians or apologize for the books of the Bible. Apologetics is an old fashioned word merely meaning those of us who have studied the Bible are explaining the faith of Christianity and the truth of the Bible to those who haven't studied.

If all of the books regarding the truth of Scripture (the Bible) were stacked on top of each other, they would likely reach the moon. Much too much information for this small study. **However, if there is one telling fact that rises above all others and is the most convincing that the Bible is true, it is fulfilled prophecy.** The Bible contains over 2,500 prophecies, most of which have already been fulfilled. Those not fulfilled relate to the end days (the seven year Tribulation), the Millennium (the thousand year reign of Christ on earth), and the return of Jesus to this earth to rule and reign for those thousand years; which, of course, hasn't happened yet.

There are over 300 prophecies relating to the birth, life, death, and resurrection (rising from the dead after He was crucified) of Jesus alone, all of which have been fulfilled with the exception, again, of those relating to His return to earth in the end days.

We see in Isaiah 7:14 the fulfilled prophecy of the birth of Jesus:

> "Therefore the Lord Himself will give you a sign: Behold, the virgin shall conceive and bear a Son and shall call His name Immanuel (meaning, God with us)."

Another prophecy of the birth of Jesus is in Isaiah 9:6:

> "For unto us a Child is born, Unto us a Son is given; and the government will

be upon His shoulder and His name will be called Wonderful, Counselor, Mighty God, Everlasting Father, Prince of Peace."

Both of these prophecies were made some 700 years before the birth of Jesus.

In Isaiah 53, we see the prophecy of who Jesus is; why He came and how He was to be afflicted and crucified to pay for the sins of others. Psalm 22, also describes His crucifixion in greater detail. In Zechariah 9:9, some 500 years before the birth of Jesus, there is the prophecy of His entry into Jerusalem on a donkey, and again in chapter 11, is the prophecy of Judas selling Jesus for 30 pieces of silver. In Micah 5:2, written some 700 years before the birth of Jesus, we see the prophecy of His birth in Bethlehem. There is neither room nor time in this small work to list all of the prophecies which have been fulfilled, however, there are numerous books on the matter which can be had at most Christian book stores.

No other book written for any other religion, nor any other book for that matter, can make the claim of fulfilled prophecy. Some people want to refer to the writings of Nostradamus, but he was an apostate priest involved in the occult and astrology and his prophecies were an obscure vague mishmash of incoherent sayings, which people have twisted to try to make it mean anything they want to imagine.

It was interesting to note some time back that there was a list of so called modern day Prophets, Seers, Astrologers, and the like who each made ten prophecies for the coming year. Along about the end of the year when most people had forgotten what they said, it was noted by a few that every single prophecy made by these modern day prophets were 100 per cent - Wrong.

There are several other proofs that lend credibility to the Bible. One such is that when the Dead Sea Scrolls were found which had been kept in a mountain cave near the Dead Sea in Israel, it was discovered that they read word for word 95 per cent the same as the Old Testament we have today with the exception that they did not contain the book of Esther. The five per cent differences amounted to such small matters as spelling and slips of the pen. This indicates the radical care taken by the Jews in copying the Scriptures in that these manuscripts were written over a thousand years before the earliest books of the Old Testament that we now have.

It is interesting that the Bible tells us that the Jews had custody of the oracles of God and in that they have done well with both the Old Testament and the New Testament. For you see, even the New Testament was written by the Jews who had accepted their Messiah, Jesus. However, some believe that Luke who wrote the Gospel of Luke and the book of Acts might have been a Gentile (non Jew), but many others today believe he was, indeed, also a Jew.

Regarding the New Testament, there is more abundant and accurate manuscript evidence for the New Testament than for any other book from the ancient world. There are no originals of any ancient writings in that writing materials grow old and deteriorate. However, the copies of the original New Testament Bible documents, of which we have some 24,133 in all languages and something over 5,000 in Greek alone, were written before the death of many of the people who lived at the same time as Jesus.

It is believed that parts of the New Testament were probably completed within the first century from 40 or 50 A.D. to 95 A.D., which would be only something between ten to sixty years after the death and resurrection of Jesus. In addition, much of what the New Testament tells us has been corroborated by secular writers of the day, including those written by the Jewish leaders who were less than fond of Jesus.

The original book of Revelation, the last book of the Bible that was written, is said to have been written about 90 to 95 A.D. by the disciple John in his old age. The other originals were written before that, very early after the resurrection of Jesus, by men who had lived in the same time period as Jesus. Had the writings been incorrect, the people who had personally known Jesus would have spoken loudly against the books. They did not. In fact, different books and letters of the New Testament were used by Christians right away, long before they were put together in a book and made canon called the Bible.

The copies from the originals that we have are 99.5 per cent in agreement with each other and the .5 per cent tends mostly to be differences in spelling. In addition, it has been said that if all of the copies of the New Testament were done away with, the whole Bible could be reconstructed from the writings of the early church fathers.

The earliest copies of most of the secular books of antiquity were some 1000 years from the event or from the original manuscripts and instead of some 25,000 copies, there are from 8 to 643 copies of the different books extant. Yet, astonishingly, no one doubts or speaks against the other ancient writings [3]. Only the Bible is questioned by non-Christians. The fact that only the Bible is ill spoken of should give us a heads up regarding the truth of the book.

Our problem? Most of the people who accuse the Bible of being a myth or full of mistakes, are people who have never studied the book nor even cracked its covers. For a book that has so much importance for our life, it seems foolish not to at least read it before criticizing it. However, it seems the Devil, (yes, there is a Devil), whispered these things in their ear and they have believed it and carried on the gossip. A good way to check up on these gossips is to ask them to name one mistake. They cannot.

---

[3] N. Geisler, *"CHRISTIAN APOLOGETICS"* pgs 306-309.

In addition to all of the above a good way to know the Bible is true is to look at the evidence of changed lives. Scripture has incredible power to change lives. When asked if he really believed Jesus turned water into wine, one reformed drunkard stated, "I don't know about that, but what I do know is that around here He turned whiskey into furniture, and that's good enough for me."

Jesus tells us in John 8:34-36:

> "...Most assuredly I say to you, whoever commits sin is a slave of sin. And a slave does not abide in the house forever, but a son abides forever. Therefore, if the Son makes you free, you shall be free indeed."

What Jesus is talking about here is addiction. It has been proven that any addiction that exists, be it substance abuse, sexual abuse, even to murder, it will make man a slave. However, any addiction can be cured completely by coming to Jesus and following Him. What Jesus is about is changed lives. If you move the Son into your house (your heart and mind), I am totally convinced that He will cure any addiction and set you free.

Another man once said, after meeting up with Jesus, "... 'Whether He (Jesus) is a sinner or not I do not know. One thing I know: that though I was blind, now I see.'" [4]. As a sinner who has been

---

[4] John 9:25, NKJV.

reading the Bible for some forty years, this writer can also testify to a radically changed life and that "though I was blind (lacked understanding), now I see." In truth, the Bible is a book that is alive.

Man does not change and sin does not change. Mankind has been doing the same wicked things from the beginning of time. But neither does God change, so this alive book can be applied to the world that existed thousands of years ago as well as to us today and can also show us how God deals with those sins. He doesn't beat the sheep up for them; He can take them away if one will allow Him to do it. The principles and truths of the Bible are as up to date as today's newspaper.

One small problem that puts people off, not with the Bible, but with our thinking about books in general, is that people think they must start at the beginning of this great tome and struggle through the begets with little or no understanding of what they are reading day after day after day. Not so. The Bible is not "a book" so to speak, but it is a "library" of books put together within one cover for your convenience. One may reach in and gather up one of the 66 books by 35 different authors and enjoy the same without the guilt of cheating by going to the last page of a mystery novel to find out who the perpetrator is. However, just to comfort your hearts, after forty years of reading the Bible daily, this writer finds within the begets many old friends met within the pages of some of the other "books" of the Bible.

Another secret that a few folks miss is that there is an Old Testament (covenant or law), written before Christ's birth, and a New Testament (covenant or contract), written after His death and resurrection, both of which can be applied to our lives today. Both show us God's dealings with man and His helps to man (this includes women, too, of course).

CHAPTER 2

IN THE BEGINNING - WHO?
(GENESIS 1:1-2 AND JOHN 1:1-3):

It is not the intent here to exhaust every last tidbit within each chapter of this small study, we must leave information for the enjoyment of further readings. However, the intent is to set forth a few points from each chapter of the Bible to build a foundation for what Christianity is and a foundation for further enlightenment regarding the rest of the book as one desires to read it. It is truly astounding, but many people do not even know what Christianity is. Many think it is just another religion with a bunch of people who try to do good works and mostly lie about their sins. Not so. They do good works and they do sin, but that's not what it's all about as we shall see in the following chapters.

It has been said by a very fine pastor, now passed on, that if you want to lose your mind, just try explaining the Trinity and he was totally correct. It is here suggested that if the translators had used the word "Elohim", (the Hebrew word used for God throughout much of the first books of the Old Testament), instead of the many other names for God it would have been beneficial. However, God has many names that describe Him of which Elohim is just one. Elohim is important, because it is what God once called himself and it is the "Plural - One God".

Christians worship one God made up of three Persons; God the Father, God the Son (Jesus), and God the Holy Spirit. We call this the Trinity. As we proceed through the Bible, however, we will note that at the head of this triangle (or Trinity) is God the Father and the other two points of the triangle being God the Son and God the Holy Spirit; yet they are one God. How can this be? Well, my poor explanation is to take a pitcher of water and set two glasses beside it. Pour some of the water from the pitcher into one glass and then some into the other. What do you have in each glass? You have the same water from the pitcher. In other words, you have God in the big pitcher and you have God poured out into each of the glasses. We are told that Jesus is the very essence of God, His Father. So again, what do you have? You have one God in three persons.

We must never forget, however, that, although equal, the Son and the Holy Spirit have willingly subjected themselves to God the Father, even as we must. And why not? They think the same and they are the same. Here, we are talking about the being, thinking, Person, personality, or essence of God.

Now, why have we gone into this? Three reasons; One, because we need to prove that Jesus was also God, God the Son, and He and the Father and the Holy Spirit are one (of the same essence) and were all present at the creation. In John 1:1-3 it tells us not only who Jesus was and is, but also that He was there at creation along with God the Father and God the Holy Spirit:

> "In the beginning was the Word (Jesus), and the Word (Jesus) was with God and the Word (Jesus) was God. 2: He was in the beginning with God. 3: All things were made through Him and without Him nothing was made that was made." NKJV

Now, the question might be, why did God keep this such a secret in Genesis? Well, probably because He had a surprise for the Jews and it wasn't time to open the present yet. If we knew why God does everything, we would be as smart as He is and that is not possible.

Why does God call His Son "the Word"? Because in Greek it is Logos and has the meaning of wisdom, rationality, etc. In Hebrew it also has within it the meaning of creative power. He (Jesus or the Word) speaks for God the Father and we are to "hear Him" [5]. He is the Father's legal agent.

The second reason we are going into this is because God calls Jesus "God" in both the Old Testament [6] and the New Testament and He proves it in the New Testament by the multitude of undisputed miracles Jesus did.

---

[5] Mark 9:7.
[6] Isaiah 9:6 (among many others).

Even Jesus' enemies did not dispute that He replaced withered hands, healed the blind, made the paralyzed get up and walk, healed the leper, cast out demons, fed thousands with a few fish and bread loaves by way of creation, walked on water, and raised the dead more than once. Not only did He raise other dead, but after they had killed Him on the cross, He raised Himself up from the dead. This is called the Resurrection and there were in excess of 500 people who saw Him after He rose from the dead. But in the fury of the Jewish leaders, they said He did the miracles by the Power of the Devil rather than by the power of the Holy Spirit.

Why were they furious when He did such good things? Because of their pride and fear of the loss of their power over the common people and because the common people listened to Jesus gladly and the Jewish leaders had the green sickness called jealousy. In addition to this the Devil was in them and they had no sense, because they listened to everything he whispered in their ears. But mostly, they hated Jesus because of their jealousy that the common people were gathering to Him.

God tells us that if we do not believe in Him, He will make us stupid [7]. It is obvious that the Jewish leaders, (along with others who did not believe in Jesus), had become stupid. They had even forgotten the prophecies of His birth and life that they had been taught from childhood.

---

[7] See Romans chapter 1.

Before we get to the third reason, let's take on some hairy problems. One being the virgin birth. How does one prove a virgin birth? You can't watch someone 24/7. Today with DNA it would be easier, but in Jesus' day they had to take it by faith. Well-l-l not exactly. A good detective could give us some help.

One thing we must understand and that is the common Jews were terrified of God. They were so afraid that when the priest went into the Holy of Holies behind the curtain in the temple, no one else could enter there. If the priest went in with the wrong attitude or had displeased God, He was known to strike them dead on the spot. So they put bells on the bottom of the priest's robe and tied a rope around his ankle. The purpose of this was that if the bells stopped ringing for a lengthy period of time they would assume that God had struck the recalcitrant priest with a bolt of lightening and he was dead. So the purpose of the rope was to drag the dead body out of the Holy of Holies and bury him elsewhere in order not to stink up the temple.

They were so afraid of God that they took the law that God gave them and wrote over 600 additional peripheral laws called the Mishnah, just to make sure they did not trample on the rather small number of laws that God had given them. Let's say one law was not to carry a burden on the Sabbath. The Jewish Mishnah added that to pick up a rock was carrying a burden. To wear false teeth was carrying a burden. To put a pin in one's clothes was to carry a burden. One could pick up a child, but if the child was holding a rock, that was carrying a burden and one could get stoned to death for it. Such things as that. Why did the Mishnah allow one to pick up a child? Well, in all probability they didn't want to listen to the child screaming and mercy was also a part of the law. However, that is another matter.

But this is the really important part. Now, in the law in Deuteronomy 23:2 it is stated that, "One of illegitimate birth shall not enter the assembly of the Lord even to the tenth generation..." As an aside, there was a man some years ago that refused Christ's love and went away furious, because of this Scripture. How sad. This is a lesson that if there is something in the Bible that we do not understand, we need to file it away under, "awaiting further input from God" and proceed on, rather than throwing the baby out with the bath water, so to speak.

But to continue, was God being unfair? Hardly. There were several reasons for this law. "A", God had to be extremely stringent. He was trying to build a Godly nation for the world to see and follow, out of a bunch of rag tag people with a slave mentality who had been living like backwoods dufuses for four-hundred years in slavery to the Egyptians.

"B", most times illegitimate children suffer the damned of Hell as children and are usually in the way and unwanted by most of the family. Today, many (more than we would think) illegitimate children are sexually molested by the mother's new husband or boy friend. God, in His kindness, wanted to put a stop to such pain that these children suffered, so He had to make the law very harsh. As the Baby Boomers used to say, "no pain, no gain". They've kind of gotten away from that lately.

"C", God wanted the people to know that the temple, like God, was holy. The congregation were also supposed to be holy and set an example for the rest of the world in order to win them to God. He wanted no sinfulness in the temple. God is not mean. The child was certainly able to pray and worship in the court of the Gentiles, but not with the congregation of God who were all supposed to be priests to the world; even as preachers today are supposed to set an example. God wants us to be holy as He is holy. If the illegitimate child's heart was right with God, God would take him in and give him a place in His kingdom, which He did many times in the Bible. The child would not be left out, because God had promised to be a Father to the fatherless.

But the last and real reason is the most important. As a Bible detective, we found out that God gives us "signs" so we can figure out the things He wants us to know. Mary, the mother of Jesus, was from a very poor sort of backwoods town. She was probably from about 12 to 16 years old, uneducated, and although very moral and godly, she was probably somewhat gentle and timid. It is more than doubtful that this woman, who was a child herself, would have dared to take an illegitimate child into the temple. Knowing God's proclivity for striking sinners dead, she would have been terrified to do so.

But we see that the very first thing she did after His birth was to have Him circumcised on the eighth day, according to the law, and when her purification was over, some 33 days later, she took Him to the temple to present Him to the Lord and the congregation as the law provided. If Jesus had been illegitimate, she would have fled so far from the temple that no one would have been able to find her or her child and in all probability we would never have heard of a man called Jesus. This would seem to indicate that she knew He was virgin born and that He was Immanuel (God with us). We might add to this that Joseph was a Godly man, probably a good deal older than Mary, and he went along with Mary to present Jesus to the congregation. This would indicate that he, too, was aware of Jesus' virgin birth [8].

Now, continuing to the third reason proving that Jesus is God the Son, that we left behind some paragraphs ago, it is to let us know that without Jesus, Christianity would not be unique. It would be just another set of rules like the many religions or paths to what other religions call Nirvana/Heaven, or the place where, so called, "good" people go when they die.

---

[8] Matthew 1:19-25.

Now that we have given probably sufficient evidence that the Bible is true, that Jesus is God the Son, and that He was there at the creation, let us look at the difference between all other religions and Christianity. All, yes every last one, of the other religions of the world, tell us that we must be "good" or do "good" or follow a set of rules they have set out and earn our way into whatever Heaven they espouse by keeping them by our own pure grit or power.

Jesus, on the other hand, tells us that we have no power; all the grit in the world won't get us to Heaven; only God is "good"; and that there is no way on God's green earth that we can ever, ever earn our own way into Heaven. Why? Because we are a fallen race and bankrupt of any good to pay our way to Heaven [9]. This will be explained later as we get into Genesis 3.

So what's the answer? Well, since Jesus is God's Son, we ought to listen to Him. In John's day the Jewish leaders were so intent upon the fact that no man could become a god (quite true), that they entirely missed the point that God might take on flesh and become a man in order to help us out. Jesus once asked Peter, "Who do men say that I, the Son of Man am?", to which Peter answered that "they" were saying he was John the Baptist returned from the dead or one of the prophets, etc., but Jesus insisted, "But who do you say that I am?"

---

[9] "The heart (of mankind) is deceitful above all things and desperately wicked..." Jeremiah 17:9.

to which Peter replied one of the most beautiful sentences in the Bible, "You are the Christ, the Son of the living God."

This God/Man and Son of God the Father, Jesus, came down to earth, took on the flesh of a man in order to live a sinless life (in our behalf) and end up dying on a cross (taking our place there) to buy our worthless skin (along with our soul and spirit) back from slavery to Satan.

You see, as will be explained later, we are all born into slavery and owned by Satan, because of sin. In Hebrews 9, the Bible tells us that without the shedding of blood, there is no forgiveness for sin. Only the sinless blood of God was the price demanded that we may be purchased out of that slavery so that we can belong to God and no longer belong to Satan. In that all humans sin, we had no sinless blood of our own to give and thus are bankrupt and unable to buy ourselves off of Satan's slave block. Again, only as we get to Genesis 3, will we be able to understand how we came to belong to Satan.

So, if all of the other religions are correct and I have to be "good" continually, or sinless continually, keep a bunch of rules, and work hard to earn my way to heaven by pure grit, I am indeed lost forever; because, you see, I cannot keep all of those rules; the Jews could not keep all of those rules; and I, along with the rest of the world, cannot stop sinning, day in and day out.

If you think you do not sin, beloved, just try not to think a bad thought about anyone or anything for even one day. Have you ever wished someone dead? Jesus tells us if we have, we are a murderer even if we did not follow through and kill the person ourselves.

You see, sin begins in the heart, not always necessarily what we do. If you want to have sex with someone you are not married to, but have not personally done it, you have already done it in your heart and you are just as guilty as if you had done it in the body. When you think of these things, you will see how weak man's so called righteousness becomes; so Jesus died for us to give us His righteousness. No other leader of any other religion has ever done that or even makes that claim. It's a deal no one should pass up.

To clarify, Jesus came so that if we believe in Him we may put on His robe of righteousness which covers us completely. We have no robe of righteousness ourselves and the robe of our own good works we try to put on isn't long enough to cover up our nakedness (our sin). It is His robe of righteousness we need that we may have (eternal) life in His name.

Another indication that Christianity is far different from any other religion is when was the last time you heard Buddha's name used as a curse word? Or Allah or Confucius or any other supposed deity? God and Jesus are the only Deities whose names are so blasphemed. This alone ought to give one a heads up and make him pay attention. Why? Because Satan hates God and His Son, Jesus, (and you, by the way) and wants you to blaspheme their names in order that he, the Devil, can take you to Hell with him when he goes there.

To continue with the proofs that there is a God, let's take a look at God the Father. To proceed with our point, "In the beginning God ...", there is not much sense in spending a lot of time trying to prove that there is a God in that He tells us in the Bible that we have been given evidence for the truth of His existence. One, He tells us that if we don't believe in Him we are a fool (crazy or empty headed [10]); two, if we don't believe in Him we are probably lying[11]; and three, He has put into the heart of every man the knowledge of God and a need to worship [12] – who? - God!

People who do not believe that God exists are called atheists and atheism is illogical. It is called a universal negative and it is impossible to prove a universal negative. In other words, in order to prove, for instance, that little green men do not exist, one would have to go to every planet, star, and comet in the universe to check it out and this is impossible. By the same token, to say that God doesn't exist, one would have to search the universe and even beyond to make sure He doesn't exist, and

---

[10] Psalm 1:1 & 53:1.
[11] Romans 1:18.
[12] Romans 1:19.

again, this is impossible. So to say He does not exist is illogical.

It was interesting to note that when some atheists were put on a lie detector and asked if they believed there was a God, their answer was "no". However, the lie detector machine jumped all over the place and found them to be fibbing just a teeny bit.

Why do people not want God around? Well, either they have been taught incorrectly and need to be educated or they are doing something that God does not approve of and they either will not or cannot give it up. So in order not to be driven crazy by guilt, they comfort themselves by telling themselves that there is no reason to worry, because there is no God anyway.

So what does one do when he either will not or cannot give up his vice? There was once a woman who wanted to come to God, but couldn't get her life in shape to do so. She promised herself that she would start following God when she got her life straightened out.

She had been misinformed. We do not straighten up our own lives. We must come to God in prayer; tell Him we are sorry enough for our sins to want to quit doing them (it's called repenting); and let Him clean us up. If we could do it ourselves, and we cannot, Jesus would not have had to come to earth and die on the cross for us.

Then there is the person who doesn't want to give up his comfort blanky (his comforting sin). If he wants to go to Heaven, that person has to go one step further back to square zero instead of square one. He has to ask God to make him "willing" to be willing to give up his security blanky, the sin he cannot do without. God rejoices even when someone wants to be willing to be willing.

CHAPTER 3

CREATION? OH GOOD GRIEF, HAVEN'T YOU HEARD ABOUT EVOLUTION?

(Genesis 1:3-27 & John 1:4-10):

Now that we have given you a scattering of pretty good evidence that there is a God, Jesus is who He said He is, and the Bible is God's Word to us, we will proceed on to another sticky wicket.

We won't go into this brouhaha very deeply in that there are a number of more than excellent apologetic writers who have made this their life study [13]. We do, however, have a few points to make.

Before we get into "were we created or dropped on a rock", we need to take a couple of things into consideration. One: if one should see a high rise building and have the sense God gave a pin headed turkey (the second dumbest animal on earth), he should suspect that somewhere off stage their lurks an architect in the wings.

By the same token since the discovery of DNA, we learn that there is enough intelligent information in each cell of one person to fill up a library of roughly 4,000 books. Now, if one should see a library of 4,000 books filled with intelligent

---

[13] See "Suggested Readings on apologetics" at the end of this study.

information, He should have just a teeny suspicion that somebody with intelligence had produced that information. It didn't just pop up out of no where.

However, no matter how intelligent they appear to be, the evolution crowd seems to go bonkers when confronted with creation and God. Sir Francis Crick, the discoverer of DNA and a Nobel prize winner can't face the idea of God and creation. Although he knew that DNA was far too complicated to have come into being by way of Darwin's silly theories, he had to find another way even if he had to refer to the funny papers. His answer - the earth was "seeded" biologically by aliens sent in rocket ships who returned to wherever they came from never to be seen again. The next question should be, then who created the aliens? It would be rolling on the floor hilarious if it weren't so serious.

Believe it, a monkey sitting at a typewriter for a million years will never write the great American novel and a Tornado in a junkyard will never produce a 747 [14]. By the same token, there is no way this well put together complicated world could have just happened.

Why is this so serious? In the mid 1800's, Darwin, a God hater and atheist, had set himself to destroy Christianity, along with the college Higher Critics (Liberals) in Germany (their colleges were full of Liberals, too). These also hated God. These so

---

[14] See "Tornado in a Junkyard", by James Perloff.

called Higher Critics, cut the Bible up, especially regarding creationism, tore out what they didn't like and by the time they were finished, there wasn't anything recognizable left of God's word. Between those two groups, the Higher Critics and the Darwinists, they have succeeded in ruining Europe and finally, now America. You don't think America is ruined? Who else could murder over 40 million pre-born infants and consider themselves righteous?

Hitler, Stalin, Mao, Margaret Sanger (the instigator of abortion), and the Liberal Left were and are all Darwinists. Today those who run the schools, colleges, government, and the media, are also mostly Darwinists. This should be an indicator of the seriousness of the evolution problem. If evolution isn't true, we have turned the mental hospital called earth over to the inmates who are ruining us and our children for generations to come.

Simply put, Darwin's theory was that things evolved slowly over millions of years, by means of mutations, until one thing finally evolved into another (called macroevolution). That "other" was then considered to be the survival of the fittest. Macroevolution, of course, is the jumping of "kinds", cat to dog, fish to bird, etc. His problem was that he had tunnel vision. What he was observing was microevolution, the ability of a bird or a moth to use other information from their inborn DNA to be able to deal with their environment. God thinks of everything, doesn't He?

In other words, certain moths have it within their DNA to change color in order to hide themselves, for safety's sake, within their environment. If this is not clear, let's assume that moths need to fit in with their environment so the birds will not eat them all and make them extinct. So within their DNA is the ability to change color when their environment makes it necessary. This is much like a chameleon who has it coded within its DNA to be able to change color to fit in with the color of his environment for safety's sake. For safety's sake even a man who lives in a tropical climate usually has the DNA coded into him for darker skin in order to protect him from the suns rays which can give him cancer and a multitude of other problems connected with the sun beating down on him constantly.

From this and other like anomalies Darwin changed the world from belief in God and creationism to hedonism and belief in a primal "soup" that brought forth one celled life which *mutated* into the world of today. That was some jump.

The problem is that mutation does not add to DNA, it takes information away and is never beneficial. In opposition to Darwin's theory, we would not have the ape to man scenario or history, we would have man to ape, because in mutations, we lose information, we do not gain it. Even some manmade mutations in flowers may lead to better color, but at the same time lead to loss of the perfume of the flower. We see this in many roses of today, beautiful to look at, but with no aroma.

Some mutations are meaningless, but most are lethal. Darwin, himself, claimed that if these *slow mutations* did not exist that his theory would not hold water. Dr Michael Behe, a biochemist has written a book called *"DARWIN'S BLACK BOX"* [15] in which he indicated that the biology of the human body was so complicated and so many processes needed to come together at the same time and so quickly that it left no time or room for Darwin's gradual mutation theory.

If Darwin's theory were true, the patient would have died before the mutations could work up their end result. So what do we have? Darwin's theory does not hold water, as he himself testified, yet most people in America believe this lie from Satan and we still teach such tripe to our kids in school. Many (but not this writer) wonder why the Darwinists insist on hanging on to their ignorance.

Another problem with Darwin's theory is that he stated if there are no "missing links", and there should be millions of them, his theory, again, falls through the cracks. Missing links are unusual species that existed between the primordial soup and the world of today such as a fish with one leg as he proceeds to evolve into a ground animal or a fish with one wing as he evolves into a bird, and such as that. But there are none, nil, not any, not

---

[15] See "Suggested Readings", end of this study.

any time nor place. Scientists keep trying to find them, but they do not exist. Oh, let us repeat that. THEY-DO-NOT-EXIST, even though the young innocent minds of school children are still taught this lie.

May God have mercy on us for allowing our children to be indoctrinated in these terrible lies in the public school system.

In Genesis 1, God, Who knows the truth, continually repeats the phrase, "after its kind" or "according to its kind". Nowhere in all of creation has it been shown that anything, from man to animals to plants have ever jumped from one "kind" to another "kind". Any husbandman can tell us that animals do not breed outside of their "kind". Some even have a hard time breeding within their kind such as the horse and the donkey. They are both equines and can breed, however, their progeny, the mule, is sterile.

Even plants will not jump "kinds". If one grafts an apple branch onto a peach tree, both the branch and sometimes even the tree, will soon wither and die. One can graft, again, according to kinds; such as many different types of peaches on to one tree and the branch will each bear the peach of its kind. However, they are all still peaches.

Thus one may have five different kinds of peaches grafted on to one tree, but you cannot get a five peached tree from planting any of the seeds of the fruit from that tree. It will revert back to its "kind" and, if it grows at all, it will bring forth only the one kind of peach. Each peach type must be grafted individually all over again for each such tree. Even a peach has DNA that says, "this is what you are going to look like, what you are going to taste like, and you will not breed with something out of your kind." One wonders who told the peach these things? I'll bet it was God.

Today men are experimenting with grafting man's DNA into an animal's DNA. Most of these are a failures. However, one such pig, when human DNA was grafted into the pig's DNA, the pig became very large; but it was also terribly diseased and soon died. You see, those horror movies about mutants were right after all. Mutants are sick and ugly. Scientists and faint hearted clergy want to say the Bible isn't a scientific book. However, It is suggested that it is definitely a scientific book, in that it is always correct when it speaks regarding scientific matters.

When God says, "after its kind", He means "after it's kind", not after another kind. One thing does not morph into another, no matter how many millions of years one has to work with or make up stories about. Man did not start out as an amoeba, become a fish, then a bird, then a monkey, then a man. Man started out as a man; the amoeba started out as an amoeba, the fish started out as a fish; the same with the bird, then the monkey. They began that way and they will end up that way. Maybe God did this so that when one planted a corn seed, one could be assured that he would reap an ear of corn. By the same token, when a pregnant woman gave birth, she would not have to be afraid that her young would sprout wings and fly out of the window of the hospital before she could get it home.

Another aspect of evolution is that the ape to man skulls that are exhibited today are frauds. Nebraska man, touted to kids in school as our ancestor ape man, was found to have been created from a pig's tooth. Not the whole pig, mind you, but merely its tooth. Piltdown Man, Java Man, Peking Man, all were apes and deliberate hoaxes. And on it goes.

Why? Because if archeologists do not "discover" their funds will be cut off and they can't have that, so every once in a while they "must" find something, anything, to keep the funds rolling in. Did God not tell us that mankind was wicked? Ah, indeed He did. By perpetrating this lie, our children are taught they are nothing but animals, so that is what they act like, little animals. They fornicate on every street corner (so to speak) like dogs and teachers complain that they can't teach them anything in schools, because it is impossible to control them. People who do not believe in God cannot be controlled long enough to teach them anything. This is just one of the results of the teaching of evolution.

Why does man let these lies continue? Genesis 3, when we get there, will explain it all, but in the meantime, let it be known that you may be a monkey's uncle, but I have definitely been made in the image of God, and I am not a monkey's uncle, however, from time to time, I do have some doubts about some of my relatives.

But what does God say? God spoke the universe into being by His Word, Jesus. And, as some honest scientists will tell us, every living thing appears to have come into existence at one very short period in time. Animals, people, etc., all appeared, zip, in one short period and there they were. There is absolutely no scientific evidence of any long drawn out evolving of anything. In fact, even scientists today have begun to tell us that we all came from one pair of parents, one man and one woman. Some scientists even call them Female Eve and Male Adam.

In Genesis 1:1, God created (bara/created out of nothing) the heavens and the earth and everything on the earth. Here we see the Holy Spirit hovering over the earth much like a mother hen hovers over her young for protection and, some say, to energize the earth.

There are some sticky points here to make, but first let's look at an orderly and common sense God. Everything was created and prepared in an orderly fashion as would be needed by man, before man was brought on the scene. How God must have loved man that everything was prepared beautifully for him before He brought man into being.

On the first day as God began preparing the earth for its inhabitants, He brought forth light, and divided it from darkness. Man and animals, as well as some plants, need darkness in order to sleep or rest. Because we are in a time continuum or we exist in time with bodies that need rest the darkness provides down time for us to rest; while daylight provides an atmosphere that encourages work or activity.

An interesting point here is that there is, as yet, no sun or moon. How then do we get light? If we look at the end of the Bible, the book of Revelation; in the New heavens and new earth there is no sun, but God and Jesus will be our light [16]. It is also interesting how a loving God is preparing a comfortable place for man that is well suited to his needs.

On the second day God created the firmament (interstellar space). Many people think the firmament is merely the earthly atmosphere (sky). However, if we look at verses 14 through 18, we note that the sun, moon, and stars are located in the firmament, which would indicate interstellar space.

It appears that earth was born of water much like babies are today. As God divided the waters it appears that the water above the firmament puts a water barrier around the universe (interstellar

---

[16] See Revelation 21. It speaks of this in verse 23, however, it is well to read the whole chapter to get the sense of it.

space). The water under the firmament (God is speaking of water in and around the earth here) may have been divided up into lakes and rivers on earth, water under the continents, and a sort of canopy of moisture in the atmosphere of the earth. Probably a mist, fog, or clouds. It is interesting that the Bible tells us that God hangs the clouds in the sky on nothing. It is also interesting that clouds hang there, upon nothing, many with tons of water in them.

Many Bible teachers want the water above the firmament to be the canopy within our atmosphere. However, they haven't read far enough to see that the water above the firmament is above interstellar space. But evidence would indicate that there must have been a see-through moisture canopy somewhere within the atmosphere of earth in that there seems to have been a protective shield that existed before the flood. Today many worry constantly about global warming, however, this protective shield of water caused global warming and the greenhouse effect which caused the following conditions [17]:

>   1. The earth was essentially uniformly pleasantly warm all over the world, allowing for a greenhouse effect and animal

---

[17] See Walter Brown, PhD, *"IN THE BEGINNING, COMPELLING EVIDENCE FOR CREATION AND THE FLOOD"* Center for Scientific Creation, Phoenix, AZ, 2001, pgs 85-119. And Henry M. Morris, (1996), *"THE GENESIS RECORD"* Baker Book House, Grand Rapids, MI. Pgs 60&61.

life at both the North and South Poles. Many warm blooded animals have been found at the North Pole frozen with lush tropical foliage still in their digestive tracts.

2. Windstorms would be inhibited, because of the uniform temperatures.

3. Warm temperatures and adequate moisture would have been conducive to the lush vegetation all over the world. There would be no barren deserts nor ice caps.

4. A vapor canopy would have filtered out ultraviolet rays, cosmic rays, and other destructive energies from outer space which would have partially accounted for the great ages of the antediluvian (pre flood) peoples and would have contributed to the health of the population. (It also must be considered that that early in creation the gene pool would have been clean of disease and other things in opposition to the health of mankind.)

5. These waters would have been laid up for the later world wide flood, along with the waters under the continents. The split of the earth during the flood would have shot these waters skyward causing the extended rain time and causing the division of the America's from Europe and the great rifts that are seen in the ocean floors today.

Yes, there was a worldwide flood. Although the Darwinist scientists want to date their fossil finds by where they appear in the strata. They also want to date a strata by where they find the fossils in it. Is this the chicken or the egg argument? The problem is that fossils are found everywhere, in all strata and many are even jumbled into animal "graveyards" from every age. What would cause this? Why, a world wide flood, of course.

Proceeding, we see that an orderly and common sense God prepared the land, that brought forth the grass, herb (vegetable fare) and the fruit trees in preparation for food for the living beings. Before the fall of man in Genesis 3, both man and animals were vegetarian. There were no animals eating other animals and no death until man brought it into the world by his sin.

Then God hung the heavenly bodies in the sky for signs, light, seasons, and growing things, etc., fish in the seas, birds in the air, and then on the sixth day, when everything was ready, He brought forth the warm blooded living beings. First the cattle, beasts of the field, creeping things, etc., then as the topper of all, the crown of creation, and for whom it had all been created, He created man.

It is interesting to note that although there are as many stars as there are grains of sand on earth, in Genesis 1:16 God tells us that, "He made the stars also." and with a wave of His hand He dismisses them and moves on to man which will be the subject of the whole rest of the Bible, both Old and New Testaments. This would indicate that God is not overly interested in "things". He is interested in us. Our children might be different if somebody would tell them that God is interested in them.

When God had finished with the big picture, it is said that, "God saw everything that He had made and indeed it was very good..." and He made it for you and for me and for our children. Although mankind has almost ruined God's creation with our sin, this world is still great. What a marvel it must have been before man fell.

While God the Father was setting forth information about the big picture in Genesis, Jesus was setting forth the more intimate picture in John 1:4-13. In Proverbs 8:31, Wisdom, which we take to be Jesus, tells us that He rejoiced in God's inhabited world and "My delight was with the sons of men." We see in John 1, that Jesus, as well as the Father, had the ability to give life within Himself and with that life came light, (intelligence); the ability to communicate with God, appreciate beauty, and the ability to have understanding. Animals cannot communicate with God nor do they have understanding. Only man is the possessor of those things. You have never seen a dog look at a sunset and turn around and say, "Hey, man, that's rad."

However, although Jesus is the light of the world, we see in John 1, verse 5, that the Bible speaks of darkness. Since the fall of man, that light was taken away from mankind and he has lived in darkness of one kind or another for thousands of years. Although the light of Jesus keeps shining, man does not appear to apprehend or comprehend His light. We cannot grasp it nor understand it, because our spirit has died within us. This leaves us in darkness until we come back to God and that light is at least partially restored to us when we ask Jesus into our hearts.

In John 1, verses 6 and 7, we see John the Baptist (not the writer of the book of John) who came to wake up mankind and prepare the way for the light to come into this world. That light is Jesus. John the Baptist was preparing the way so that we might believe in Jesus when He showed up.

It is a sad commentary on mankind that the very Person who created them was not known to them. Especially the Jewish nation who were called "His own" and who had been briefed beforehand by the word of God, the Bible. They did not know who to look for. However, miracle of miracles, there were a few of the Jewish nation who recognized Jesus for who He was when He came to earth. Those who recognized Jesus then and those who recognize Him today because of their words (or writings, the Bible), and those who will receive Him and believe in His name, are given the authority to become adopted children of God the Father with all of the benefits and inheritances of Jesus.

In John 1:13, Jesus indicates that just because you have experienced natural birth, and you are merely the everyday fallen man, you will not make the grade. In other words, that will not get you into heaven. Many people think that if they were born in America that makes them a Christian. Not at all. Just because one lives in a doghouse, does not necessarily make him a dog.

Jesus tells us we *must (it is imperative that) we* be born of God. That is God, himself, must raise our spirit from the dead. The disease that mankind has is a dead spirit. All men are born with a dead spirit because when Adam fell into sin, he passed the disease of a dead spirit on to all of his children. Our spirit is that part of us that can communicate with God. He must put into our hearts and minds the truth about Jesus and return that original light our first parents had in the Garden of Eden. We must have a change of heart about just about everything we have ever thought we knew in the past. It is also imperative that we know that we cannot do this ourselves. It must be done by God. How can we get God to do this for us?   We ask.

John the Baptist then tells us that Jesus is the (final) Lamb of God. The Passover lamb (an animal) was slain in order to liberate the Jews from slavery in Egypt. After that liberation, lambs were to be continually slain in the temple in Jerusalem to liberate the Jews from their sins. However, the slaying of an animal only covered up the sins of man, it didn't take away the sins of man. Now, He, Jesus, will be slain in the place of the lamb, once and for all mankind, to liberate us from slavery to Satan and our sins, and to bring us into fellowship with Him and into the family of God in Heaven forever. The slaying of Jesus on the cross did not just cover up our sin, it took it completely away as far as the east is from the west.

It's like the bus to Sheboygan that is driven by Jesus. You get on the right bus and Jesus will take you where you need to go. You can trust Him. An interesting aside is that in 70 A.D., after the death and resurrection of Jesus, the Jewish temple was destroyed. Why? There are several reasons, but the main one is that since Jesus had made Himself the sacrificial lamb, the temple was no longer needed in order to slay lambs for the forgiveness of sin.

CHAPTER 4

IN SIX DAYS? YOU'VE GOT TO BE KIDDING
(Genesis 1:3-27):

Your question? How can the earth have come into being in six days when the scientists tell us it took millions and some say billions of years for the world to evolve into what it is today and besides, the stars are millions of light years away proving they, the evolutionists, are right? Right?

Sigh....One thing we must all remember is that scientists are also humans; they also have religious presuppositions such as evolution (yes, evolution is a religion albeit atheistic); and that science has a half life of about five years. What this means is that within five years, about half of what they have told us today will be obsolete and tossed into the trash can. Scientists do not have all of the answers, because they do not have all of the information yet. In fact, they don't even have all of the questions right.

For instance, since Einstein it has been proven that light does not always travel in a straight line. How about that, huh? In grade school and art school it is taught, even today, that light always, always and double always travels in a straight line. No, it can bend, go around corners, and do all sorts of strange things in space. How do we know? Well, Einstein, and other scientists have said so. What does that do to the light years it takes for light to travel from a star in space to earth? I have no idea and neither, by the way, do the scientists. We are here into quantum physics, the great guesswork trash can of the scientific world. Continue and we shall see.

Add to that we now know that time is not the same all over the universe. In fact, time is not the same all over the earth. Time will be different between a valley and a mountain top, not even taking into consideration the time and date lines on earth. Here we can get lost in the Schwarzschild Coordinates indicating the varying times throughout the universe. Not being a physicist we will not go into this, but suffice it to say that time on earth is much faster than time in space and as one reaches the ends of interstellar space time slows down almost to a stop. This is why scientists are now beginning to speculate that a person can leave earth, fly around in space, and come back to earth the same age they were when they left, or nearly so, while the earth has aged dramatically. We must remember that we live in a time continuum and God is in charge. However, God does not. In His Heaven and eternity, there is no time.

Add to this that the universe has been expanding from the time of creation and will continue to do so until the end of the world. That which was closer at creation, the planets, stars, and such, are now much farther away. In fact even today the moon is moving slowly away from earth. Dr. Russell Humphreys tells us that:

> "While the light from the most distant galaxy was traveling to us, the universe expanded by about a factor of five stretching the light's wavelength by the same factor and giving it a red shift parameter of four [18]"

What are we getting at? Dr Humphreys is telling us that while a few days were passing on earth, billions of years would have been available in space for light to travel to earth.

By Einstein's theory of "General Relativity" we now know that we must ask, "Six days as measured by which clock?" All of this may account for a good deal of the light year argument of the evolutionary scientists. However, not being a Quantum Physicist nor Astrophysicist I am not able to argue in depth about it, but it does give us insight into the fact that no longer is it "proven" that the earth and the universe are billions of years old merely because a star or planet appears to be several million light years away.

In that the universe is expanding, it didn't start out that far away to begin with. Second, in the beginning the smaller universe would cause time to be massively distorted. Taking into consideration that both light and time are not constant and both have done and still do strange things out in interstellar space, astrophysicists will need to do a

---

[18] *"STARLIGHT AND TIME"* By D. Russell Humphreys, Ph.D., pgs 123-126.

lot more studying before taking a stand on the age of the universe let alone, whether it could be created in six days.

One can "decide" what the age of the universe is based on whatever so called "facts" they have "decided" to take into consideration; however, it doesn't prove a thing; especially if there are a few hundred other scientists who have "decided" upon another set of so called "facts" to come to another conclusion.

Taking into consideration that the itinerary (the Bible) is always right, let's take a look at what God has to say about it. I take it He is more believable than the astrophysicists, in any event. Let's take the word "day" in the Bible. The word "day" (the Hebrew yom) occurs in the Bible approximately 2,182 times. It can mean a 24 hour day or it can also be used to denote a specific designated occurrence or period of time, such as "in the day of the Lord". However, in over 95 percent of the cases, the word for day in the Bible indicates a literal 24 hour day.

In addition, when the word day is associated with a numeral, as it is over 200 times in the Old Testament, it invariably means a literal 24 hour day. In Genesis 1, we have not only numerals attached to the word "day", but we also have the phrase, "evening and morning" which would further nail it down to a literal 24 hour day. I take it that God wanted to hammer it into our thick heads that He created the earth in six literal days. I hope your

God is big enough to have created the world in a nano second, mine is. However, we note with gratitude that in His loving care, He took a full six days to do it right.

IN HIS IMAGE

CHAPTER 5

THAT'S M' BOY

(a parable) (Gen 1:26 through 2:25):

Mac had a kid that was the apple of his eye. You could hear Mac all over town bragging about his boy. "Look at that kid's feet" he would say with an embarrassed grin. "Big as mule's hooves, just like mine." "Look at that cowlick stick up. He looks just like me." and he would turn around and show you his cowlick. There was nothing Mac wouldn't do for that kid. Every time you saw Mac going down the street with a big smile on his face, the kid wasn't far behind.

Then one day it came time to send the kid off to college. Mac didn't want him to go away, but he had scrimped and saved every penny to give the kid the best there was. He had enrolled him in the most prestigious college in the state. The first year the kid came home for every vacation; Christmas, Easter, summer vacation, and Thanksgiving. While he was gone, Mac didn't smile so much, but the shiny grin came back in all of its glory every time the kid came home.

The next year and the two years after that the kid just couldn't find the time to come home and he decided to go "with the guys" for his summer vacations. Mac still bragged about the kid, but he didn't smile as much any more. After graduation the kid got a job with a large and important firm and Mac seldom heard from him. Then the kid was busy getting married and raising a family and the time came when Mac hadn't seen the kid for years. One day Mac got hurt from being in an accident, but the kid didn't even call to talk to him.

Then one day Mac's kid got arrested for embezzling money from his company and was about to go to jail for the rest of his life. He lost everything, his home, his wife, his kids. He called Mac and told him what had happened and Mac sold everything he had, even pulled out his retirement and paid the debt; got the kid out of jail, and tried to talk to him and get him to come home and start over. Well, the kid wouldn't listen and he finally ended up on skid row and then one day someone shot him as he was robbing a convenience store. It's funny, not funny ha ha, but funny strange, that after the funeral, Mac went home, but he never smiled again.

The Bible tells us in Job 38:7, that the angels sang when God laid the foundations of the earth. But after the fall of man, you never hear that the angels ever sang again. They would "say" and "speak", but they never sang. Maybe it was a reflection of their Master's grief.

> 26 "...Let Us make man in **Our** image, according to **Our likeness;** let them have **dominion** over the fish of the sea, over the birds of the air, and over the cattle, over all the earth and over every creeping thing that creeps on the earth." 27 So God created man in **His own image**; in the image of God

> He created him; **male and female** He created them. 28 Then God blessed them, and God said to them, 'Be fruitful and multiply; fill the earth and subdue it; **have dominion** over the fish of the sea, over the birds of the air, and over every living thing that moves on the earth.'" Gen 1:26-28 NKJV

God created man just like Himself and then He gave him dominion (rule) over everything.

God said, "...Let **Us** make man in **Our** image, according to **Our likeness."** This would, again, indicate the plurality that God speaks of. We note that the "image" of God, "Our image" appears to be one image, that of the Father, the Son, and the Holy Spirit.

And to these children, he gave "dominion". They ruled. They were King Adam and Queen Eve. God gave them the whole universe to look at and the whole world to rule. You want to do this when you have a "kid" that you dearly love. You want to give them everything.

One anomaly of Bible literature is the "repeat". That is that God will tell us that He did something, then He will tell more of the story, then return to the first subject and tell us how He did it. This is true of the creation of man/woman. In Genesis 1:26, He tells us that He created "him" and then He tells us He created "them". Then He proceeds with more of the story and in Genesis 2:7, He gives us a bit more information about Adam's creation; then in verses 2:18 through the end of chapter 2, He explains all about Eve and the wedding.

If you want to know how much God loves you, take a second look at Genesis 1:26 through the end of Genesis 2. Like Mac, God made man in His own image. Just like Himself. Have you ever looked at your kids and seen yourself in their face, hands, feet? Didn't it make you grin and love them more?

Man was the crown of God's creation for whom everything else was created and God was proud of him/them. But how are we made in God's image? He has no body, because He is Spirit. Well, God is a Trinity, and so is man, of sorts. God is Father, Son, and Holy Spirit. We are body, soul, and spirit. The soul is where we think. It is our personality, it is the "me". The spirit, man's spirit, is where we communicate with God who is Spirit and it is what makes us "alive".

When our spirit is dead, we are considered dead by God, because we can no longer truly communicate with Him nor understand anything about Him. We live in darkness, if you will. You will hear non-Christians tell you that they don't like nor believe in the "God of the Old Testament". They only want the God of love, the one in the New Testament. What they don't understand is that they do not know God at all, because the God of the Old Testament is the very same God as that of the New Testament. In fact, the reason they have no understanding of God at all is, because unless one's spirit is brought to life by God (being born again), it is not possible to know or understand God.

Man is eternal. When we die, that is not the end. The decision of where our new body, soul, and spirit take up their abode is decided today, while we are here on earth. Know that at the end, even our renewed body will be raised again to join our soul and spirit. This life is a test that makes the decision do we go to Heaven or Hell? We know that Heaven is a grand place, but what is Hell like? It is full of pain; physical, mental, and emotional. The most awful thing about Hell is that there are no "pain pills" there and it never ends. We are not akin to the animals who have a different flesh and possess only a body and soul (personality) both of which come to an end when they die. No, like God, mankind will go on forever.

Man has a sense of guilt when he sins and has a developed consciousness of judgment to come. Animals do not have this capacity. Man can worship, read, write, and has language skills. He can communicate. He can accumulate achievements from one generation to another. He can set long term goals, cook his food, make clothing, invent elaborate tools. Man, like God, has a moral and spiritual nature. Man alone can appreciate beauty and has a hope for immortality beyond the grave. God transmits His secrets to man, never to an animal. Man stands alone in that he calls God "Father". Man stands in the place of a son. Man alone has the capacity to know the mind and will of

God. Why? Because he was made in the image of God. Being made in the image of God is not what one looks like, it is what one is able to know.

And like Mac, God loved his son/daughter, Adam/Eve and gave Adam and Eve everything on earth. There were stars to gaze at, a sun and moon to give light, darkness, warmth, and joy. He gave them a day of rest and, in the Garden, man was given six days of work that was not burdensome. Despite what people think today, work gives us something to do. Without it we would be continually bored and depressed. Even God works until today. However, Adam's work in the garden was not difficult. There were no thorns, thistles, nor weeds. No sweat. He didn't have to do things two or three times to get it right. And best of all, he could stand tall and young. He didn't have to be bent over with age and the pains of age. Much of his work may have been the mere speaking of a word.

In addition to fruit bearing trees, there was pure water from a river that became four rivers. There was gold there. Not just any gold, but the best gold and jewel stones. Then God gave him a companion. His attitude when he saw her was one of shouting joy when he said "this is bone of my bones and flesh of my flesh". It was an attitude of "wow, she's gorgeous." And she was also man - wo -man or out of man. Surrounded by all of this beauty and sustenance of paradise, there was only one fly in the ointment, so to speak. One rule. God told Adam:

> "Of every tree of the garden you may freely eat; but of the tree of the knowledge of good and evil, you shall not eat, for in the day that you eat of it you shall surely die."

God knew that tree, that it was a bad tree. Just like God knows what will hurt man on the earth today and so He makes rules to try to protect man. But does man listen? No.

God knew that the AIDS virus and sexual diseases were sneaking around on the earth waiting to catch men and that promiscuous sex between both men and women and men and men could spread it and kill us and infect and kill our children. So He made a rule, no sex of any kind outside of marriage. Have one partner and let anything else go. God was not against sex. He invented it, but He loves us and just wanted to protect His children and His children's children from suffering, disease, and death put here by Satan and caused by the sin of man. So He said, "don't eat of that tree." As we look at the morals of man today, we can plainly see that that tree would never be safe with man around. Don't you wish God had drowned it in Round-up? But it wouldn't have helped. Like the Devil, it would have sprouted up in a million other places.

God is not arbitrary. If one looks at the ten commandments, one can plainly see that not keeping them will cause pain to somebody, and mainly to the person not keeping them. Do you hate your neighbor because you want what he has? Friend, it will eat you up. What about adultery? It always hurts somebody, if not with disease, then with emotional pain. I guess an unfaithful mate is one of the most heart breaking things on earth. It can mark one for the rest of their life.

Do you steal? Someone put out some hard work and sweat to get what he has. Why should someone who refuses to work for their own things kick open your door and take what you have? How about a false witness? More people have been ruined by the lies of someone else than the world will ever know. And on it goes. There is good reason for every law God ever made if we were just to stop a minute and take a look. But no, we are rebellious and bull headed. It is born within us. God is not a cosmic killjoy. He is doing something in your life that is going to turn out for your good. God is into the "good" thing. He tells us in Romans 8:28, "And we know that all things work together for good to those who love God, to those who are the called according to His purpose."

Believe it or not, there are some marriages that are "very good". However, they take place between those who love God and have put away selfishness from themselves. They are the people who do not do the fifty per cent thing: they are into the 100 per cent thing each. Before the fall, Adam and Eve were into the 100 per cent thing, giving all they had to each other and walking with God and their marriage was "good". In fact, it was perfect. As we proceed, we will see what the "fall of man" did to marriage.

As we proceed to the wedding of Adam and Eve, we have a very interesting passage, that a man shall leave his father and mother and be joined to his wife and they shall become one flesh. In that Adam didn't have an earthly father and mother that he should leave them, we gather that Genesis was written about Adam, but it was written for us. To all mankind, just like the rest of the Bible.

Probably more marriages have been broken up by in-laws, the husband's "buddies", and the gossip of the wife's girl friends, than for any other reason. As far as marriage is concerned, the only interference God allowed was Himself. Adam's wife was programmed to be his best friend. She was programmed not to bad mouth her husband to her girl friends and so should it be between a man and his wife today. She should be the one that watches his back and his kids and he should be the one who provides for and protects her and the kids. And never, never should he call her "the old lady" or any other demeaning name nor should she call him "the old man". She was made to be his beloved other half, not his adversary. God tells us that a man's prayers won't even reach the ceiling, let alone heaven, if he mistreats his wife.

So we see that God loves a wedding and it is sacred, because it was His first act in dealing with His children. Jesus, His Son, also loves a wedding and loves us so much that He likened the church

(Christians) to being His bride. If one looks at a Jewish wedding in Jesus' day, one will see that the groom proposes to the bride, then he goes away to His Father's house to prepare a place for His bride. In John 14:1, Jesus tells His disciples:

> "Let not your heart be troubled. You believe in God, believe also in Me. In My Father's house are many mansions. If it were not so I would have told you. I go to prepare a place for you."

As soon as the bride's place is ready, the groom returns to the bride's home with his friends to take her to her new home. He may come at any time and the bride must be ready to go to the wedding feast. But we, the bride, are warned to "watch" for we do not know what hour our Lord is coming. He may come to get us when we die or we may be caught up to heaven (raptured) and meet Him in the clouds before God's wrath is poured out on people who refused to come to Him. So He warns us not to get too involved in the things of this earth and to keep our eyes open and "watch" for His coming.

CHAPTER 6

GOD LOVES A WEDDING

(John chapter 2):

The book of John, chapter 2, is a most heart warming chapter of the Bible and here we will pick out just a few points of interest. Point number one is that Jesus has quit carpentering. By now His stepfather, Joseph, has undoubtedly passed away and His brothers were old enough to take over the family business. At about the age of thirty, He is now going to begin to be about His Father's business, the business of explaining about the Kingdom of God to those who are interested.

It seems that about three days after Jesus began gathering His disciples, along with His family and His disciples, Jesus is invited to a wedding; a thing we know He loves. A wedding is a joyful occasion and the first one was put together by God the Father, Himself, in Genesis chapter two.

As we attend this wedding along with Jesus, it is interesting to note that virgins were usually wed on a Wednesday, while widows were married on a Thursday. In either event, weddings usually lasted a full week and the host was responsible to provide wine for all guests for the full week. It appears that Jesus' mother has a position at this wedding of helping out the family and lo and behold they have run out of wine. Now, this was a very unfortunate occurrence in an Israeli wedding; somewhat akin to inviting your new boss to dinner only to discover that you have forgotten to turn on the oven and the roast, which takes about three hours to cook, is still raw. About this time the doorbell begins ringing announcing the arrival of your guests. It is a total disaster.

Now, many people want the miracle in this chapter to be the first one that Jesus did while on earth, the one to open His ministry. However, there are a couple of interesting points that might dispute this belief. This may have been His first public miracle, but it is suggested that if He hadn't done miracles within the family, how would Mary have known to go to Him with her problem?

Jesus is, by now, merely a poor itinerant preacher. He had to borrow a coin later to explain about Roman taxes to the disciples of the Pharisees [19]. There was no way He could have run down to the corner winemaker and picked up a couple of gallons of wine. Mary knew where to go when she needed a miracle and she was perfectly comfortable with it as she told the servants, "Whatever He says to you, do it." This is also good advice for us, whatever Jesus says to us, we need to do it. If we do as Jesus says, our life, like that wineless party, will not end in embarrassment.

It appears here that Jesus was hesitant and wasn't quite ready to start His public ministry, but the circumstances rather pushed Him into it. He speaks to His mother, telling her that His hour had

---

[19] See Matthew 22:15-22.

not yet come. Was He speaking of His hour to start His public ministry which would be the first step on the way to the cross and death?

Now, there were six stone water pots available, which held about twenty or thirty gallons of water when filled. They were used for the ceremonial washings practiced by the Jews. It was a matter of the legalistic cleansing of the Jewish religion that when one had mixed with Gentiles (those dirty unsaved non-Jewish rabble) in the market place or before meals one would put their hands in the water, hold their hands aloft, and let the water run down to their elbow and turn the hands down again, letting the water drip off their finger tips. The water could also be used in an immersion pool for ceremonial cleansing.

Actually, the Jews were ignorant regarding what they were "chosen" for. They thought they were chosen to be the spoiled children of God. However, Jesus had really "chosen" the Jews to go to the world and tell them about His Father, God; but as one can see, they thought themselves better than others, because they were "chosen" and they treated the Gentiles with contempt rather than love. In fact, in the market place, a Jewish Rabbi would pull his clothes close around himself so they would not touch a Gentile (a non Jew) by accident and thus defile himself.

To fill these water pots with anything but clean water would defile the jars and render those old jars useless. However, we see that Jesus is about to make some badly needed changes in their form of worship and He disregarded the problem when He told the servants to fill the water pots with water, about 120 to 180 gallons, and they filled them to the brim. Let us never say that Jesus doesn't provide for His own in abundance.

At this time the servants were told by Jesus to dip some of the "water" out and take it to the master of the feast (a sort of head butler) and let him taste it. The feast master had no idea that this was water turned to wine and he exclaimed that it was the best wine. Most people serve the good wine first and then when one's taste buds were deadened, they were served the cheaper wine. But this wine was proclaimed to be better than what had been served before; the best wine.

There are two lessons here. The main one was that Jesus was giving us a picture of what He had come to do. He had come to replace the dead watery legalistic Jewish religion with Joyful newborn Christianity. Wine is a symbol of joy. He came to bring the good news that the Kingdom of Christianity was at hand and all of the old laws that even the Jews couldn't keep were going to be done away with. Actually the laws would be fulfilled by Jesus so they could be done away with. It was the "new covenant."

No more slaughtering of lambs, He was the last Lamb of God. He would die on the cross for our sins, once for all. Not to merely cover them up as was the case with the slaughter of the Passover lambs; but He would be the Lamb slaughtered to put our sins away from us as far as the east is from the west and He, Himself, would become a ladder for us to climb into Heaven and God once for all. Of course, this was written for us in that the Jews, even the disciples, didn't understand what He was doing until much later.

Jesus later elaborated on the new wine in that it could not be put into old wineskins or it would be too much for the old wineskins (the old religion). It all had to be new; new wine into new wineskins. The born again experience and the Holy Spirit into the new move of God, Christianity.

The second lesson was that as the feast master tasted the wine he found it to be the best wine. When Jesus does a miracle for you, and He does them daily, you can better believe **He cares enough to give the very best.** The joy of Christianity **is** the very best. There is no way we can keep the rules and regulations of all of those other religions. There was no way we could keep all of the laws in the Old Testament and enter Heaven as perfect people. The Jews couldn't do it then and neither can we do it now.

There is no way any of us can keep from sinning today, yesterday, or tomorrow; so Jesus was going to give His sinless blood to buy us back from Satan, raise our dead spirits back to life, and give us His perfection by way of His white robe of righteousness. It is only with His wine (a picture of His blood) and His robe of righteousness that anyone in the world can enter Heaven.

Jesus tells us in John 14:6, **"I am the way, the truth, and the life. No one comes to the Father except through Me."** Now, here is where we fish or cut bait. We either believe Him or consider Him a liar. No other choice is left open to us. Do you think He is just a "good man"? No, if he is a liar, He is not a good man. So when He tells us there is no way to God the Father and Heaven except through Him, it is imperative that we listen.

Jesus is our knight in shining armor. He came to rescue us and take us by the hand and introduce us to the Father as one of His. Just imagine you were before a Judge in a court of law and your lawyer was found to be the Judge's only beloved Son. Well, we are told that Jesus is our advocate, our lawyer, and like the parable about Mac above, God loves His Son with an undying love and He loves us the same way, because we were created in His image and because we belong to Jesus. That is, those who have asked Jesus if they can belong to Him.

As we close out chapter 2 of John, we see Jesus, meek and mild? Not at all. He is our warrior. He announces who He is by driving the money changers out of the temple with a whip. This house (Temple) was His Father's house and it was to be a place of prayer for all nations, yet the Jewish leaders had made a house of thieving merchandise out of it and it infuriated our Lord.

It was the law that the animals that were presented for sacrifice to the Lord were to be without blemish. They were to represent Jesus who was without sin and without blemish. It seems that not only were the Jewish leaders overcharging for the animals they sold to be sacrificed, but they always found a flaw in the ones the poor brought from home; forcing them to spend their hard earned money to purchase a temple animal. Not only that, but the regular civil money could not be given in the temple, because it had an image of Caesar on it making it an idol. So they had to change their money for temple money with no images on it and in doing this they were charged an inflated fee for the exchange. The Jewish leaders were cheating God's people coming and going.

Secondly, this market took place in the court of the Gentiles, the only place in the temple where the Gentiles could pray to God, those very people to whom the Jews were supposed to minister. In Both Isaiah 42 and 49, as well as Acts 13, the Jews were told that they were to be a light to the Gentiles. It was just another indication of their hubris and their contempt for both God and the Gentiles that they turned the court of the Gentiles into a thieving market place rather than a quiet place of prayer.

Here Jesus accomplished two things. He let them know that He knew what they were up to, and He used this as a way of getting their attention. It didn't make them like Him any better and finally they murdered Him for it, among other reasons; but from now on they would know who they were dealing with.

CHAPTER 7

THE PROBLEM

(It surely must be God's fault): (Genesis 3:1-10, Isaiah 14:4-17, and Ezekiel 28:12-19):

There are so many people who want to blame everything on God. Why does God let this happen or that happen. Why does God allow wars. Why does He allow suffering and on and on it goes. Well, the answer to all of these questions lies in Genesis chapter 3. It is the pivotal point of the Bible. Without Genesis 3, no other chapter of the Bible would make sense. In fact, without Genesis 3, even the world as it now exists would be senseless.

In Genesis 3:1, we are introduced to the trouble maker of the universe. "Now, the serpent was more cunning (crafty, subtle, shrewd, slick, deceitful and satanic) than any beast of the field..." And why not. The serpent was a beast that had allowed Satan to inhabit and use his body for evil. Yes, there is such a thing as Demon possession.

It is interesting to note that our arrogant, and educated elite of America sneer at the idea of Demon possession. If they lived in many other countries of the world, they would find possession to be frequent and obvious, but here in America the Devil has chosen to work underground. He has decided that he can accomplish more in this so called arrogant educated country if he merely whispered into the ears of a people who do not believe he even exists or if he does exist, he is merely a powerless comic character. In other words, many are possessed and are doing Satan's work without even being aware that they are doing it. Such an incident was true in John 13:27, as Satan entered Judas and programmed him to sell Jesus out for thirty pieces of silver.

There are several other Scriptures that recognize that people serve Satan by possession. Looking at Ezekiel 28:12-19. In this passage we note that Satan is up to his old tricks. At first it appears that God is speaking to the King of Tyre, however, God is really speaking to the power behind or within the King, that person who is programming the King to do his will. Satan is the real, though invisible power behind many successive rulers of the world. We can see this in the very next verse. Here God indicates to whom He is speaking by nailing it down to "You were in Eden, the Garden of God..." Now, Eden was destroyed hundreds of years before the King of Tyre was even born, so we know God was not talking directly to the king, but He was talking to Satan, the power behind the throne.

Then we are told how beautiful Satan was. He was covered with jewels and that he was the great musician of Heaven right from the day he was created. We learn that he was the anointed Cherub who covers. This is an indication of the great power and place that this great prince had in the presence of God. It seems there is a place of fiery stones where God walks and he was allowed to walk there also. He was top dog, so to speak among the angels. However, we need to know that God did not create the Devil (the accuser, slanderer, demon, the greatest of all fallen spirits), He created a perfect personality called Lucifer (light giver, brightness) who was perfect until iniquity was found in him. What was that iniquity? It was pride and the coveting desire to replace God. He coveted God's power and God's throne.

We come across this person again in Isaiah 14:4-17. Here again it appears that God is speaking to the King of Babylon, however, it is the same scenario as with the King of Tyre. We see in verse 12, that God begins to speak directly to "Lucifer", son of the morning. To know how great this being was and is we need to look at Lucifer, created to be an angel of light in Heaven.

Satan was not created evil, he became evil through pride and of his own free will and that is what God is all about, free will. God is not a jailer. He wants free people. Satan took advantage of God's kindness and freedom and when he did, he took one-third of the angels of heaven with him. Today those are the demons who trouble man continually and cause all of the troubles of the world that we keep blaming on God.

God took a chance putting the Tree of the Knowledge of Good and Evil in the garden, but, again, Adam and Eve had free will. It was a test, a choice. Do we listen to God or do our own thing? Were they competent to have dominion over everything? They could choose to eat or not to eat just as we have "choices" today. Maybe abortion is our tree of the knowledge of good and evil in this age and that is why a woman has a "choice" as to whether to kill her child or not. Choice is what it is all about. Your choices can kill you or save you.

God is not the God of mechanical wind up dolls or slaves. He is the God of freedom. He does not want you to be forced to love Him and be obedient to Him. He wants you to be free to choose to love Him and in loving Him you will be obedient, because you will know that He has only your best interests in His heart.

In Genesis 3:1-2, it is interesting to note that Eve is talking here to a snake. It doesn't bother her nor appear to surprise her that this snake can talk in that she seems to converse with him quite comfortably. This might indicate that in the Garden, the animals, or at least some of them, could talk.

As we look at Genesis 3:1-5, what was Eve's very first mistake? Why, listening to Satan to begin with. Jesus tells us that Satan is a liar and the father of lies. No matter what he says to you, it will either be a lie or a half truth. A half truth is like drinking what you think is a clear glass of water, but without your knowledge a few drops of arsenic have been dropped in when your back was turned. Satan comes and he acts as an angel of light with just the right words you want to hear.

Beloved, when things look dark for you and you think that God has forsaken you, remember who it is who lies. God does not lie and He has said that He will **never** leave you nor forsake you and He has put it in His book to show you that He does not change His mind. So if you are hearing another voice that is telling you that God is so angry with you that He has left you, remember who it is who lies. It is definitely not God. God can be trusted.

Eve's second mistake was talking back or arguing with Satan. Let it be known that Satan is a great intelligent and powerful prince. He loves to play games. There is no way you can out argue him nor best him at his game. He knows what he is doing and he has been practicing for thousands of years. Your best bet is not to play games with him at all. Your only, and wisest, recourse is to immediately turn him off and turn him over to God. Call on God immediately. Sad to say we don't always get it at first when he is talking to us. We think it may be God or even our own mind talking to us. This is also what makes him so dangerous, because the battles with Satan begin in the mind.

One always wants to warn people. When anyone tells you that "Everyone is doing it" (whatever "it" is), beware, you are listening to the Devil who is in that person and the longer you argue with that person, the more easily he will convince you. All of a sudden you will begin to think, "well, it doesn't sound so bad." Again, you are listening to Satan and this time he is within you. Satan loves mind games.

Does he tell you everyone is stealing from the company, having sex outside of marriage, aborting your child when you have had sex outside of marriage, cheating on your taxes, cheating a cashier at the check out stand? And on it goes until we are forced into a corner and can end up doing murder. If you do not believe this, remember David in the Bible. He began by merely taking a day off from work. It was spring and he didn't go out to war in the spring as was the custom of kings in those days. He stayed home and ended up in adultery and murder.

Satan always begins with small sins and when one has fallen for that, he backs you into a corner inch by inch until you can't get out and you do a really bad thing that you may have to live with for the rest of your life. Did you start out addicted to dope, cigarettes, or alcohol? Not at all. It was just a pinch of fun. Try it out. Then soon you couldn't put it away from you.

The truth is that we have an innate conscience. We know right from wrong and we probably knew it was wrong when it was just a little sin, even though we would deny it. If we can take it to God when it is a little sin, He can put a stop to it before it becomes a big sin.

Satan lies as he whispers in our ears. Jesus calls him the father of lies. Today Satan's big lie is that Christ is not the one and only true way to God. However, we have been blessedly born in a country that if one looks at our history and listens to God and the Bible, he will know that Satan is whispering this lie into our ear. God tells us that the work He demands of us is to believe on Him (Jesus) whom He has sent. And for some this is indeed hard work when Satan continually whispers in our ears that Jesus is not the way. Remember, Satan lies. It is his very nature.

Let's look at the progression of Eve's sin that began in the Garden. The serpent whispers, "Has God indeed said..." The first thing Satan does is cast doubt. He casts doubt on God and then on you. "Did God really say something so dumb?" Or "Did you really hear Him right?" Satan loves doubt. It is his most effective weapon against mankind, because it makes one question the truth that we really know or should know. First we should not suspect it is God talking to us, because God is succinct. Look at the ten commandments. "Thou shalt not..." It is clear and leaves no questions in your mind. On the other hand, Satan likes to fog the issues.

Next he stretches the truth. "Has God indeed said 'You shall not eat of **every** tree of the garden'?" Every tree? God didn't say that or anything like that. Here Satan was being ridiculous, because if they couldn't eat of any of the trees they would starve. God, in fact, created the trees for their fruit which was food for those living on earth. Here Satan blatantly accuses God of doing them harm and denying them even the food they need. He tells us that God is not being fair; that He wants to cause you to be hungry, etc.

Always remember, God has promised to take care of us and provide for our needs. Not necessarily our greeds, but out needs[20], if we seek first the Kingdom of Heaven. We can see how desperately important it is to know what God has told us in His word, the Bible. It is the only way we can overcome the lies of Satan. In fact, it was the only weapon Jesus used against Satan when He was on earth. Every time Satan tempted Him, His response was, **"It is written..."**

In Genesis 3:2-3, Satan has gotten exactly what he started out to get. He wanted Eve to argue with him and try to protect God and indeed she does. Well, God doesn't need our protection and arguing with Satan is a useless game, but she fell for it. Now that you know, don't fall for it. She should have sent him packing the minute he came into her eyesight or she should have left the minute he opened his mouth. God tells us to flee. Get out of there when Satan is talking to you.

Eve adds somewhat to what God told Adam about not eating the fruit of the tree. She adds that they are not even to touch it and some people fault her for that. However, I'm not so sure that was a bad thing. Although we are not to add nor take away from what God tells us, however, most times it is the better part of valor not to even be in the vicinity of a forbidden object. In any event here it appears that she is acting on second hand knowledge. The Bible doesn't tell us that God told Eve directly

---

[20] Matthew 6:32-34.

about the tree, but He told Adam and it was, no doubt, passed on to her from him.

There is probably more danger in second hand knowledge than almost anything else on earth. Returning to the bus trip to Sheboygan above, did the man who made it to Sheboygan listen to the ticket agent? He did not. He read the itinerary for himself. Do you listen to every "preacher" you hear, or do you read the Bible for yourself to find out if he knows what he is talking about? If you listen to *every* preacher without checking him out with the Bible, you are in danger of getting on the wrong bus every time. There are religions out there that claim Biblical authority, but they have rewritten the Bible, removed parts of it, or are not telling you the whole story. There are many preachers in good denominations who do not believe the Bible themselves.

There were a group of people spoken of in the book of Acts called the Bereans[21] whom the Bible called "more noble". The reason? When they heard Paul preach, they went home and read the Bible to see if what he was saying was true. We need to read the Bible daily to make sure we are not being taken in; to make sure we are listening to the right ticket agent, so to speak.

Next, in Genesis 3:4-5, Satan tells an outright lie. When Eve tells him that if they eat of this fruit they will die, Satan tells her that God is lying to

---

[21] Acts 17:10-12.

her and that she surely will not die. Not only are we all going to die because of the sin of Adam and Eve and our sins, too, but when we sin our spirit dies right away and we can no longer hear God nor do we even want to. God told us, and He cannot lie.

The last lie was the biggest. Satan first makes God out to be jealous and hateful and then he promises Eve godhood. And why not. It was the very sin that trapped him. He wanted to be god. He knew it would also trap a less intelligent being like Eve.

There are religions today that tell you if you follow them you will one day be a god. Run the other way as fast as you can for you are in the midst of Satan's den. You are not a god and you will never, never be a god nor an angel nor any other heavenly being. You are a human being, a creation of God Almighty and that is what you will always be.

You must let that sink in so that you will never be taken in by Satan's lies or so called churches who propagate such wickedness. Some religions lean on a Scripture wherein Jesus said, "...I said you are gods..."Small "g". However, the ancient connotation here is "judges" not "Deity". Judges act in the place of God in that they have power over your life, however, they are not deity (and they need to remember that). This scripture is also an indication that if they do not handle the job of judging properly, they will ultimately answer to God who **is** Deity.

In verse six, Eve begins her walk to death. She begins to contemplate the tree. She didn't just glance at it, she contemplated it. Stood looking at it for a long while letting her mind take it in. It is called the lust of the eyes. If you are on a diet and you stand outside of a donut shop and contemplate the goodies in the window, what will happen? Once it progresses that far you are lost. You will be in that donut shop not even realizing you have entered the door. If you begin to "contemplate" any sin, there is no longer any hope for you. It is the last step just before going over the cliff.

If you have a romantic "thing" for the boss and you can't get your eyes off of him/her, what do you think will be the result? Before you know it you will go to lunch with him, then dinner one night, and soon you will be in his bed wondering how in the world you got there.

God tells us that sin is crouching at your door and it desires to have you. See sin as a being, half animal, half person, with bloody pointed teeth, crouching like a lion at your door, ready to spring at you and murder you. Sin is said to be pleasurable for a short time, then the bitter dregs lie at the bottom of the glass you are drinking from, waiting to trap you and poison you. Sin must be nipped in the bud. Once it has become a flower you are an addict and then a dead person. If something evil attracts you, turn your eyes away and do-not-look-at-it. Close your eyes and flee. It is the lust of the eyes and it will trap you completely.

Sexual sins are especially vicious generally causing disease and/or the break up of marriages. This writer once worked in divorce court in Los Angeles and it was the most violent court in the county. Men have been sentenced to death in criminal courts with less uproar. There were more suicides, murders, knifings, gun fights, and fisticuffs than in any other court in the system. This cannot be stressed enough, sin kills. If it does not kill your body, it can kill your spirit, separate you from God and send you to Hell.

And where was Adam when all of this was going on? Many think he had gone wandering around the garden, but Scripture tells us that he was **with her** and he ate. Adam had not left her there alone with the enemy, he was "with her". When you pick your friends, remember that sin always loves company. Bad friends corrupt good morals. Bad friends will always, not sometimes, but always, cause us to fall. Eve ate and she gave it to her husband and he also ate. She wanted company in her sin and Adam acquiesced.

Here we must explain the circumstances of this sad act. It was with their disobedience to their God that they forfeited their dominion. They were no longer King Adam and Queen Eve. It was here that Satan won dominion by default over the earth away from man. How do we know? Let's take a look at Luke 4:1-13.

Here Jesus has gone into the wilderness to be tempted by the Devil and in verse 5 Satan shows

Jesus *all the kingdoms of the world* and he (Satan) said to Jesus,

> "All this authority I will give You and their glory; for this has been delivered to me and I give it to whomever I wish. Therefore, if You will worship before me, all will be Yours."

Jesus then said to him:

> "Get behind Me, Satan! For **it is written**, 'You shall worship the Lord your God, and Him only you shall serve.'"

Here when Satan claims ownership of all the kingdoms of the world, Jesus does not argue with him in that He, Jesus, knows it is true. In fact that is why Jesus had come, to buy back those kingdoms and His people with His blood. And what a temptation. Jesus has had to come to earth to undo what Adam and Eve had done, by dying a bloody death on the cross. He has to withstand the temptations of Satan in our behalf. Do you think He was not tempted? He knew that the kingdoms would one day be His, however, He would have to hang on a cross and die to win them. Here Satan was offering them to Him without suffering. It was temptation alright, but Jesus did not listen to Satan and, unlike Adam, He did not fail the test. If we are ever thankful about anything, this ought to top the list, because it made a way into Heaven for us.

In Genesis 3, in addition to the loss of dominion because of their sin, Adam and Eve must die. They will die physically some 900 years later, which wouldn't have happened had they been obedient, but their spirit died immediately. They will no longer have the same access to God the way they had from the beginning. No longer would they have access to the garden or to walk with God in the cool of the evening. No more would they have the peace of innocence, but only the constant prickle of guilt that would follow them the rest of their lives. In addition to this they inherited a disease called sin (a fallen nature) that would be passed on to mankind until the end of the world.

God tells us that we are, because of the acts of Adam and Eve, "inclined to evil". This means that all mankind, because of this pivotal act, is slipping and sliding down an incline trying to hold on for dear life to keep from sliding right into Hell. In verse seven guilt overwhelms them and they try to cover up the nakedness of their sin by way of sewing fig leaves together. Then when God comes into the garden looking for them the first thing they do is hide. And that is the story of every sinner and atheist that lives today. They hide from God and their guilt, because they either can't or won't give up their sin. They refuse to talk to God in prayer. They tell everyone that He doesn't exist or that He is cruel or that He doesn't care. Those who are merely repeating Satan's lie do so to alleviate the awful sting of guilt that they must live with.

So when we decry what goes on in the world today, don't blame God. The blame goes first to Adam, because he sinned and next to us, because we also sin, and then to Satan, because he is now the one who is ruling the world. Oh, yes, the world still belongs to God, but by law, Satan gets to run it. In fact, if God didn't curtail Satan's activities, things would be much worse than they already are.

And how much worse are they today? As we jump ahead about 6,000 years we can see much of the culmination of Satan's rule. Today we live in a world that is being manipulated by groups of power hungry men. Assemblages of men called the Bilderberg Group, the Trilateral Commission, the Council of Foreign Relations, the World Council of Churches, and even the Skull and Bones group out of Yale. Most of these groups are godless and occult. Many of the men who belong to each of these groups may also belong to all of them, because they work together and are all seeking the same ends.

This study is not a political treatise in that we have other fish to fry, but if you want to know more about these groups, what they do, and who belongs to them the internet has reams of information; more information about them than you ever wanted to know. However, you had better get it quickly, because, as you know, the government is trying to monitor and tax the internet. This move is probably more about monitoring the internet than it is about taxing it. After all, an uneducated people are usually a slave people.

Do you believe you are running this country? That your vote counts for the different federal political offices? Maybe, but probably not as much as you might think. Most of the time, but not always, these groups of men have already chosen their man to fill the higher offices; not only for this country, but many other Western countries, also. The man they choose will follow the instructions given them by these groups and America and the world at large will be manipulated to follow the man who is following the instructions of the groups.

What do these men want? They want money and power and will use any means at hand to get it. They will consort with Satan, murder, and any other thing that comes to their minds. They want to rule a one world religion and a one world government with a small elite at the top and make the rest of us either petty officials of their government or slaves. They want to turn America into a third world country. They **do not** want freedom for the people; countries run by Constitutions; and most of all they don't want God and His Son, Jesus to even be spoken of.

If you do not believe this, remember every word that has been said about separation of church and state and know that this is definitely not in the Constitution of this country. It is in the constitution of another failing country called Russia, but not in America. These organizations have their fingers into 4 power areas of manipulation; politics, banking, education, and even religion. Regarding religion, much of it started with the World Council of Churches. Many people leading this organization do not believe in God, the Bible, nor in Jesus, the Christ. To belong to the World Council of Churches, you may believe just about anything you want to believe, with the exception, that you cannot believe that Jesus is the only way to God. Most of these organizations listed above began in about the mid 1800's and following and family after family of these elite groups have carried it on since. You will see within the groups the teachings of Darwin and the rest of the Liberal clap trap we hear in our world today such as abortion, homosexual marriage, and the like.

The next question is, does it matter that these groups are on the way to ruling the whole world? The answer to that question is, probably not much - but only if - you are a Christian. You see, God has a plan, He has a time line, and He has promised to take care of His own. The fact is that men like this have existed since the fall of man, beginning with the son of Adam, Cain, who began his rebellion by messing around with religion.

Can these men be stopped? Not by us, but they can be slowed down and hampered in their power hunt. There is a story of how people can waylay the actions of these men and slow them down. In the 1930's, the Government started the Social Security program and gave everyone a number. The people of that time were totally immersed in a Bible culture and when they heard that they were going to be "numbered" they screamed so loud that the

Government finally made a law that the number could not be used except for the purposes of getting retirement money to the holders of the number. In fact it was illegal for anyone else to even ask for the number.

Because the people were going to "get something", namely money, they finally gave in and took the number and today, despite the law that it is illegal, every organization files all of your information by use of that number. If someone else has your number, they can even steal your identity. It is your number for life and you will never get rid of it. You cannot even do business without it.

The questions are, why did the people in the 1930's scream about the number and the people today say nothing? Two reasons! One, the people in the 1930's were Biblically literate. They knew God and believed what God had told them was coming and rose up in wrath to protect themselves. Two, the people today do not know God, they do not know their Bible and they do not know what is coming and how being numbered even comes into play.

As we read above, Satan told Jesus that all the kingdoms of the world had been given into his hand and he could give them to anyone he wanted. We remember that Jesus did not argue with him, because He knew it was true. But God has a time line for earth. That time line takes in a period called the church age which is the 2,000, plus years since the crucifixion of Christ. At a time known only by God, there will come a seven year period called the Great Tribulation. It will be the worst time the world has ever known or will ever know. It will be so bad that the only thing that will save the few men left on earth will be the return of Jesus to earth to remove Satan's reign and Jesus will rule for a one thousand year period called the Millennium.

During this seven year period, the Tribulation, there will be a one world religion and a one world government ruled over by a man possessed by Satan who is called the Antichrist. He will institute a law that every person will be issued a number and without this number a person cannot buy or sell anything. If one does not have this number, he will ultimately be killed or die of hunger. Now comes the sticking point. The only way to get this number is to worship Satan and the Antichrist. However, if one takes the number, he can no longer be saved. He is bound for Hell and can never go to Heaven.

Now we can see why it is so important to know the Bible and why these good Biblically literate folk screamed and balked at receiving a number. So a knowledge of God's word and a good loud voice is, many times, what will slow the power hungry men of this world down. That's the bad side. There is, however, a good side. **As we shall see, there is one more move to the game.**

There is a story often told of a great painting in a gallery that depicts a young man playing chess with the Devil. The prize of the chess game is the young man's soul and as we look at the painting it appears that the young man is losing. He is check mated and about to lose the game. One day a chess champion came to the gallery to see the painting. As he stood contemplating the situation for a long time, his face brightened and he said "Eureka" (I have found it) or words to that effect, **"the young man has one more move."** and indeed he did. He had one more move to save his soul from Satan.

The painting is a picture of the life of each of us. No matter what our life has been, how many sins we have committed and no matter how we feel that we have lost the game forever, just remember, **we all have "one more move" and that move is asking Jesus to be our Lord and Savior.**

As we return to Genesis 3, verse 9, we see God calling out to the couple just as he calls out to so many of us today; but like Adam and Eve, most of us are not aware that we have one more move and we are still hiding from God.

Genesis 3:8

"And they (Adam and Eve) heard the sound of the Lord God walking in the garden in the cool of the day and Adam and his wife hid themselves from the presence of the Lord God among the trees of the garden."

CHAPTER 8

SENTENCE IS PASSED

(Genesis 3:11-24):

If God knows everything, and He does, why did He have to ask Adam who told him he was naked and confront him about eating from the wrong tree? Because before God passes sentence, He must always deal with our sin. Adam had to confess his sin in order for God to deal with it. We, too, must confess our sins before God can deal with them and forgive us. Even in our courts of law today, a person must plead guilty or not guilty before the court will deal with them.

What is the first thing this King Adam is doing? The most beautiful, strong, intelligent, heroic man ever created has turned into a pathetic worm who blames his wife and then even God. **"The woman You gave me..."** And it has ever been thus. Ask a man who wants a divorce; it's the woman's fault. Ask a man who is chasing on his wife. "My wife doesn't understand me." Ask a man who has trouble in life. "God hates me." Sigh...

As God confronts the woman, she blames the serpent. "The Serpent deceived me." "Boo hoo, the Devil made me do it." Was it true? Yes, the woman was definitely deceived, but Adam was not. In fact, in the New Testament Paul tells us this in both II Corinthians 11:3 and I Timothy 2:14.

Even today women are far more easily deceived than men. That is probably why we have the feminist movement, because Satan wants women out of the home so he can get at their family, their children. And, as usual, they have fallen for it. Women are continually talked into things by Satan filled men, and they still continually fall for it. Women are generally more emotional and although they do have instinctive protections, their emotions have a tendency to fog up their judgment. They are built that way, because they need this emotionalism in order to deal properly with their children. But evil men play on this weakness of woman. All one has to do is tell a woman how beautiful they are and how much you love them and true or not they all go soft on you.

Men, on the other hand, are fashioned out of tougher stuff. They must face other godless men in the work a day world and deal with them. Without a keen eye and a smidgeon of cynicism, they wouldn't have a chance out there. Women usually assume that people are telling the truth; while men usually assume that they are not. This is why it is foolish for men to leave their wives and/or put them out to work. All they do is leave them open to predators and make hard eyed feminists of them.

So sentence is meted out. First the serpent along with the Devil who possessed him. Because he has allowed the Devil to use his body, the serpent, which it seems has heretofore stood in an upright position, would, from now on, crawl on its belly and eat dust until the end of the world. Yes, even in the

Millennium the serpent will eat dust. Regarding Satan, there would be enmity between himself and the woman and between her seed (Jesus) and his seed. His, the Devil's seed, may take in Satan himself, but also the many Antichrists that have troubled the world since, including the main Antichrist that will arise during the Great Tribulation.

Then, the seed of the woman would bruise Satan's headship and Satan would bruise the heel of Christ. Her seed? Only men have seed. Woman produce the egg. However, this is the first prophecy of the virgin born Christ. It would be a child that would be born of God and the only human involved would be the virgin woman. In bruising Satan's head or headship of earth, Jesus would, by his sinlessness and death on the cross, take dominion away from Satan and then He would be King of kings. Satan on the other hand would merely bruise Jesus, because Jesus would rise from the dead three days after his crucifixion. It was a beautiful prophecy giving hope to the couple who understood it, but who now felt hopeless.

The woman, on the other hand, was sentenced to bear children in great pain and her husband would rule over her. It states that her desire shall be toward her husband which is rather foggy. Many believe the same Hebrew word for the desire of the woman was used in Genesis 4 regarding Cain when God told him that sin desired him or sin desired to rule over him. It has ever been true, sad to say, that women desire to rule over men and never more so than today. In any event, the sentence that a man shall rule over his wife has been a thorn in the side of women for over 6,000 years.

Because of the fall of mankind, generally men have not been very kind to women. In many parts of the world men will take a wife or several wives, but pray and thank God that they were not born a woman. In many parts of the world women cannot inherit and have been thought to be too stupid to testify in a court of law and too stupid to even be educated. We have Darwin to thank for much of this in today's world. He maintained that women were inferior to men in all respects, which, of course, is not true. When God created Eve, she was a helper fit for Adam, a companion. Neither man nor woman is inferior. They are different, but equal.

In much of the east women have done in the past and do today, the hard labor in the fields while men sit and commune in coffee houses. It is only in these last years that women in some countries have come out screaming at the double standards of almost every culture and have demanded their "rights". However, the main lesson here is that we now see what the fall did to relations between men and women.

Only in Christian and the Israelite countries have women gotten the better deal. They have Jesus to thank for this. Even the Jews, who were God's chosen people, allowed a woman to inherit wealth. Although the Bible does still indicate that a woman must respect her husband and be in submission to him [22] (somebody has to be the CEO); in God's eyes, all Christians are equal and they are to submit to each other and husbands are to love their wives. So many men forget about the part about submitting to one another and loving their wives. They think they get to be boss. However, Jesus tells us that he who is greatest among us shall be servant of all [23].

And in another place, men are told that they are not to be harsh with their wives. In God's eyes, to mistreat one's wife will cut a man off from God. So if any person on earth would have more reason to thank Jesus and follow Him, it should be the feminine sex. So ladies, quit burning your bras and get on your knees and thank Jesus for His wonderful benefits.

As God sentenced Adam, we see a curse that really hits home. Men are, by nature, basically lazy and here God tells the man that he must provide for himself and his family by the sweat of his brow for the rest of his life. As he labors in sweat, the ground will only bring forth thorns and thistles for him.

We see men frustrated by having to do everything twice, because few things work right the first time. They can never find the right tool to use and everything either breaks or falls on their head. It is pitiful to see a man with a boat that never works or

---

[22] See Ephesians 5:21-31.
[23] See Matthew 23:11.

he is working on it continually. Cars are always breaking down and on it goes. Generally, men hate physical work, while generally, women do not. Most couch potatoes are men and boys and in order to get something done around the house, a man must be cajoled, begged, and nagged. In fact, it is obvious that the hammock was built especially with the male in mind. When God made his sentences, He knew exactly what He was doing.

Men do not have it so good, after all. In Christian countries, men had to walk on the outside by the road to keep the mud from passing vehicles from splashing on the ladies. In taking that place, if there was danger, the danger was always to the man. Men had to go out into the woods and shoot and dress the deer while the women stayed home in the warm cabin. If there is a frightening noise downstairs, the man must go. If there is a bug the size of an egg, the man must kill it. This is all generally speaking, of course.

While it is true women have to suffer pain to get a baby, but then they are rewarded by a warm sweet thing to cuddle. Men get all of the dirty jobs with little or no reward. And last, before this generation of silly women, only men had to go to war, sloop on the ground, and slop around in the mud and be shot at. Now, these things are not all true of all situations, but they are generally true. Even as the curse for the woman is not always true in that not all women marry, nor do all bear children, but again, it is generally true.

In Genesis 3:21 through the end of the chapter, we find additional curses. One, the first thing God did was kill an animal, probably a much loved friend to the couple, to make a skin to cover the sins of the couple. The fig leaf, their own works, just did not make the grade. They had never seen blood flow nor death before. In the Garden, nothing died until the fall of man.

This was the beginning of the rule that without the shedding of blood there is no forgiveness of sin. From this time on death came into our world and someone innocent, animal or Christ, had to be slain to cover the sin of man.

Next was a mixed blessing and curse. The couple were driven out of the Garden and a Cherubim (an angelic heavenly being) with a flaming sword was placed at the gate to keep them out. It is noticed that God drove them out. They probably balked at leaving the garden where they felt safe and cared for. The curse was the loss of paradise. When we are told that crime is caused by poverty, please don't laugh in that person's face. Adam and Eve had everything in a perfect Garden, yet they sinned. As time goes on to the end of the world, there will be a thousand years of perfect life on earth called the Millennium. Yet at the very end, the world again rises up in a vicious war forcing God to destroy both the Heavens and the Earth.

The blessing was the Cherubim that barred their way to the tree of life. Had they eaten of the tree of life they would have had to have lived forever in their miserable sinful state. We have the whole Bible, they did not. All they knew was to expect a Son that was a Savior and would bring relief to their sad estate.

Today we know that in Heaven the tree of life will be restored to those who follow Jesus. How do we know that? Well, we sneaked a peak at the end of the book of Revelation in the Bible. We hate death that came about because of Adam's sin, but in a way it is a blessing. We grow old, weak, and sick and it seems it is time to leave this earth of blood, sweat, and tears and move on. So we die to this evil world, but those who follow Jesus have the opportunity to return to paradise and the tree of life forever. For the others, death is the curse of a continual Hell forever.

111

CHAPTER 9

THE SOLUTION:

(The Gift, a Parable) (John 3):

Hillary was rather young when she got her gift. It was a rag doll with button eyes sewn on, yarn hair, a plaid dress and shiny black leather shoes. Hillary hated the gift. None of her other friends had such a gift. Her mother wouldn't let her give it away or throw it away, so she kept it around. Mostly she used it to smack her brother in the head. She would grab it by the leg and swing it at him when he annoyed her. Once when her parents gave her what she thought was a bad time, she grabbed one of the button eyes, and in anger yanked it out leaving the doll with only one eye.

She was always trying to get rid of the doll. When the family went to visit someone, Hillary always tried to leave the doll at someone else's house, but somehow the gift always ended up back at home. Someone would call about the doll or bring it back to her. Finally Hillary married and left home, but she left the doll with her mother and father.

After a while, the doll seemed to be always under foot at her folks' home so that even her mother tired of seeing it and took it to the trash bin one day and finally disposed of it once and for all. The trash was picked up and sorted for first this, then that, and no one knows how it happened, but the gift finally ended up in a dumpster behind a bar in the poorer part of town. The doll kept falling out of the bin and being thrown back in until one day a shadow fell on the dumpster and it turned out to be a funny looking man with long hair, a beard, and some sort of a long coat or dress. He reached into the dumpster, picked up the doll, dusted it off, and stuck it in his pocket.

The strange man who had picked up the doll walked to a small cubby hole of a building, opened the door, and went in. Inside appeared to be a workshop of sorts. He took the doll from his pocket and took a long thoughtful look at it. Finally he dusted it off, cleaned it up, washed its yarn hair, and its plaid dress. He dusted off the shiny shoes and sewed on a new button eye. When he was finally satisfied that the doll looked especially nice, he lovingly set the doll on the mantel and went about his other duties.

The strange man was in the business, if you could call it a business, of fixing up toys and giving them to children for Christmases and birthdays. He earned no money for his work. It seems, though, that he took a special liking to the rag doll with the yarn hair and plaid dress, and decided to keep it. After so many years, the despised gift finally found a home and she remained with the strange man from that time on.

Jesus has been known to have picked up and cleaned up many unwanted rag dolls in this world. When He has finished with them they are, many times, as good as new or at least nearly so. In some, the scars remain. However, He loves them just as well and keeps them all the same, because to Him they are beautiful.

We learned above that the world is in the shape it is in, basically because of the Devil's dominion and because of the sin of mankind. Jesus calls Satan the Prince of this world. Now we must find the solution to this situation. Because God is good and He loves us, He will show us how He will provide the solution for us.

In chapter 3 of the book of John we come across, not a rag doll, but someone at the complete opposite end of the spectrum; a wealthy Pharisee (religious leader in Israel) named Nicodemus, a ruler and teacher of the Israelites. Although he was a respected religious man, he was in no better spiritual position than the discarded rag doll. Like many others in his day he was curious about Jesus; but he came to talk to Him by night, because he was ashamed to be seen in the daylight by his friends talking to an itinerant preacher who was unschooled and totally without funds.

He begins the conversation by buttering Jesus up. He calls Him Rabbi, knowing He had not been to Rabbinical school, and admits that no one could do the things that Jesus was doing unless God was with Him. But did he really believe that? It's doubtful, because if he really believed that this Man was from God, he wouldn't have come by night and he would have followed Jesus to the ends of the earth. Wouldn't you?

Jesus who was truly from His Father God and probably tired to death of the snow job Nicodemus was giving Him, cuts to the chase and tells Nicodemus, "Most assuredly, I say to you, unless one is born again (born from above), he cannot see (enter or even understand) the kingdom of God [24]." Here we see that Nicodemus is totally lost. He begins his argument with Jesus by speaking of an earthly birth, how can a person go back into his mother's womb, etc., while Jesus is talking about a heavenly birth; God raising a man's spirit from the dead.

Jesus then tells Nicodemus that he must be born of water and the Holy Spirit in order to enter into heaven (the Kingdom of God). Now, many churches consider this to be baptism by water and a new birth or understanding *about* God and *from* God. Other churches do not believe that water baptism is a "must" for entering heaven, but what is meant here is the washing by the "water" of the word (the Bible)[25], along with the new birth of understanding about God and from God. However one looks at it, **both water baptism and a knowledge of the Bible are needed and probably should be the correct understanding of this scripture.**

Let's take a look at the problem. Jesus speaks of being washed by the "water" of the word, the Bible; and He tells us that even hearing His word will

---

[24] John 3:3.
[25] See Ephesians 5:26-27.

make us clean [26]. He also tells us that we are born again through the word of God (the Bible) [27]; but Jesus also speaks of water baptism when He tells His disciples to "Go, therefore, and make disciples of all nations, baptizing them in the name of the Father and of the Son and of the Holy Spirit [28]"

In any event, one must have the new birth from God; and all true Christians subscribe to this belief. That is, as we discovered in the last chapter, that when Adam and Eve sinned by disobeying God, they did, indeed, die; but it was their spirit that died first right away; the part of them that could understand and communicate with God. Their bodies died some 900 odd years later.

What Jesus is here talking about in the new birth is that God must raise man's spirit from the dead before he can even understand what God has to say to him. In John 5:25, Jesus tells us that, "...the hour is coming and now is when the dead (in both body and spirit) will hear the voice of the Son of God; and those who hear will live." And again He tells us in John 6:63, "It is the (Holy) Spirit who gives life; the flesh profits nothing. The words that I speak to you are Spirit and they are life."

Regarding the beliefs on water baptism and the water of the word, the Bible, both are correct and both are absolutely necessary for the new birth.

---

[26] See John 15:3.
[27] See I Peter 1:23.
[28] See Matthew 28:19.

One is born again when the Holy Spirit speaks to him through the reading, or hearing, the word; and one enters into the congregation of the "saved" (heaven bound) by way of water baptism.

If one is kept from water baptism for various reasons (if he is in prison, ill, on his deathbed, or no water is available to him for some reason) one does not lose their place in heaven for this. The thief on the cross next to Jesus at the crucifixion had no opportunity to be baptized by water, however, Jesus told him that he would be in paradise with Him that very day.

If water baptism is available, however, the very first act of every Christian is to be obedient to God and do as He tells us. He tells us to be baptized by water baptism and He also tells us that we must abide (live daily) in His word, the Bible. So as we can see, again, both are correct; both are obedience to God. It is too bad that many churches do not see this dual meaning more clearly.

At this point Nicodemus, thinking in earthly terms, is stunned and asks, "How can these things be?" Whereupon Jesus is also surprised that this man who is listed as "the" teacher of the Jews, not just any teacher, was not aware of these Spiritual truths.

Jesus then tells Nicodemus some other truths, that up to now no one has been to heaven but Himself, Jesus, thus letting Nicodemus know that Jesus was, indeed, from God. And it was true. Up to this time when one died they went to the bowels of the earth wherein there were two compartments; one for the unsaved and one for the saved [29]. In John 3:14, Jesus then hints to Nicodemus how He, Jesus, would die, by being lifted up on the cross and the most important verses in the Bible then follow, from John 3: 15-16:

> "... that **WHOEVER believes in Him (Jesus) should not perish but have eternal life. For God so loved the world that He gave His only begotten Son that - WHOEVER - believes in Him should not perish but have everlasting life.**"

And again in John 3:36:

> "**He who believes in the Son (Jesus) has everlasting life (in Heaven): and he who does not believe the Son shall not see life, but the wrath of God abides on him.**"

That means whoever. Each one of us is a "whoever" and if we believe in the virgin born Son of God; begotten by God, not made (not created); that He died on the cross for our sins and rose from the dead after three days, we will not perish in Hell, but spend eternity in Heaven with Him. To

---

[29] See Luke 16:19-31.

reiterate, God tells us that when the Jews asked Jesus, "What shall we do that we may work the works of God?" Jesus answered, "This is the work of God, that you believe in Him (Jesus) whom He (God the Father) sent." [30]

Man lives forever. We are eternal beings. The question is where do we spend that eternity? God gives us only two choices, Heaven or Hell. The choice is yours to make and the time is now. We are not guaranteed even one more breath today. As the book of Psalms would say, "Selah" (stop and think about that).

We are living in a period of grace (an unmerited gift from God). Two thousand years ago Jesus came to give us this time of the unmerited (unearned) gift of salvation (being saved from going to Hell), free of charge. He paid the bill with His blood. He did not come at that time to judge us. When He returns at the end of the world, it will no longer be a time of grace, but the time of judgment. We don't know how much of this "grace" period is left, but looking at all of the prophecies in the Bible, it must end soon. So now is the time to grab the gold ring and take Jesus at His word, because it may not be available much longer.

Jesus tells us here in John 3:18, that He is the only begotten Son of God the Father and if we believe in Him we will not be condemned to Hell and if we do not believe in Him, we are condemned already.

---

[30] See John 6:28-29.

Why are those who do not believe condemned? Because the good we think we are doing may well be doing more harm than good and in any event, any good we may do by accident will never outweigh the sins we have committed in this life. However, the things Jesus did are evidence that He is not lying and that He is the only begotten Son of God, thus able to do what He said He came to do.

No other person in history has ever done the miracles Jesus did; miracles of healing, giving sight to the blind, walking on water, stopping a storm, creating food for thousands, raising the dead and even raising Himself from the dead. These are all good things from a God who is totally good.

In John 3:19, Jesus explodes the argument that all religions are the same or they are just different paths to the same god by stating that this condemnation and lack of belief in Him will come upon a man, because he loves darkness (he refuses the truth) in order to cover up his evil deeds and not for any other reason. If a man really desires to please God and do what is right, God will seek that man out even to the ends of the world and tell him about Jesus.

Many other religions allow a person to indulge in the sin they love. Christianity does not. Does God sanction more than one wife, fornication, or adultery? He does not. Does God want us to kill one another because we belong to another religion? Of course not. Does He want us to ignore the plight of the poor and those abused by others? Only those fooled by Satan believe that. The real God is a God of love. In Micah 6:8 God tells us what is good:

> "He (God) has shown you, O man, what is good; And what does the Lord require of you but to do justly (be fair), to love mercy (kindness), and to walk humbly with your God?"

The real God is just and merciful. Friend, would you really want to spend eternity with any other sort of God?

Even though Jesus clearly states that He is the only way to God, Christians are forbidden to murder non-Christians just because they refuse Jesus. Those who refuse Jesus are left to God, not the so called mercies of sinful man. Rather, Christians are taught to love those whom Satan has tricked and try to get others saved and into Heaven by telling them the truth. Christians are taught to protect the weak and disenfranchised, not abuse them.

Jesus came to give us peace from the gyrations of the many religions of the world for which we should all be grateful to Him. Gyrations are what most other religions are all about.

We can see how the darkness of man covers his evil deeds and thinking. If man wants to murder, then he will make a religion that allows him to murder. If a man wants to indulge in illicit sex, then he will invent a religion that allows that. A man's religion does not require that he do these things, rather, a man who wants to do these things will invent a religion that allows him to do what he already wants to do anyway.

All religions other than Christianity are involved in what is called Arianism (not Aryanism); which is a religious heresy. That is, those who do not believe that Jesus is the Son of God. Jesus tells us that if we do not believe that He is the Son of God, we are condemned already.

Before leaving Nicodemus and moving on with His disciples, Jesus tells him that those who do not come to Jesus, do not come because they refuse to give up the practicing of evil. We all sin, but we do not all "practice" sin. The Christian comes to the Light (Christ), repents, asks forgiveness, and forgetting that which is behind he/she struggles to move forward toward God and to obtain the righteousness from Christ that He has promised. Like a small child who is learning to walk, the Christian will stumble and fall, seven times or even seventy times seven, but he will get back up seventy times seven and continue his walk in Christ. Why? Because it is Christ who lifts him up; but the evil man falls, never to rise again.

And what about Nicodemus? Did he ever get saved (come to Jesus) (get into Heaven)? Well, it appears that he might. Nicodemus was probably a priest and priests were forbidden to touch a dead body. Especially they were forbidden to touch a dead body before Passover or they were considered unclean and could not celebrate the Passover. The next time we see Nicodemus, it is on the night of Jesus' death on the cross, three days before Passover.

> John 19:38-42:
> "After this (Jesus' death on the cross"), Joseph of Arimathea, being a disciple of Jesus, but secretly for fear of the Jews, asked Pilate that he might take away the body of Jesus; and Pilate gave him permission. So he came and took the body of Jesus. (39) And Nicodemus, who at first came to Jesus by night, also came, bringing a mixture of myrrh and aloes, about a hundred pounds. (40) Then **they** took the body of Jesus and bound it in strips of linen with spices as the custom of the Jews is to bury. (41) Now, in the place where He was crucified there was a garden, and in the garden a new tomb in which no one had yet been laid. (42) So there *they (both Nicodemus and Joseph)* laid Jesus, because of the Jews' Preparation Day, for the tomb was nearby."

CHAPTER 10

IN THE IMAGE OF ADAM

(Genesis 4):

Adam was created in the image of God; but after the fall of man, all were then born in the image of Adam with the seed of sin within them. Mark this, no one escapes.

Having been cast out of the Garden, man now lives in penury and hard labor as promised by God. A son (Cain) is born to Eve in great pain, again as promised by God. But the son she thought was the "seed" that God had promised who would rescue mankind, was instead, a bad seed. After she got to know her son, she discovered that he was not that seed that would save them. That Seed (Jesus) wouldn't be born until some 4,000 years later.

In fact, one of the first things Cain did was much like the first things all sinful men do today. When they don't like the way God runs things, they begin to start a new religion. Cain was the first to start the religion of his own "works". As we reflect back, we remember that God's religion is one of faith. Even Abraham was said to be righteous, because he believed God. All other religions were and are based upon the works of man. Cain was of the seed of the serpent and he began messing with religion very early on.

In the process of time Cain sacrificed an offering to God of the fruit of the ground, fruits, vegetables, the work of his own hands; while the second son, Abel, brought a lamb and sacrificed it spilling its blood. Here God accepted Abel's sacrifice, but spurned Cain's. How do we know this? Well, both boys well knew that there is no forgiveness of sin without the shedding of blood. God, Himself, killed an animal and took its skin to make clothing for Adam and Eve to cover up their now sinful nakedness as they left the garden.

It is obvious both boys were educated in this matter by their parents, else how would Abel have known what to do? Besides, we have further testimony in the Jewish law at a later time that only the sacrifice of blood was acceptable to God. It was a foreshadowing or prophecy of the shedding of blood of His own Son, Jesus, that men may be forgiven for their sin.

How did Cain know that his sacrifice was unacceptable? Probably because, as is shown at other places in the Bible, when God accepted a sacrifice, He sent fire down from Heaven upon the alter and burned up the sacrifice. All Cain's sacrifice did was smolder. The green sickness, jealousy, is a powerful spark toward evil. As Cain snarled and pouted in jealous rage, God, like a loving father, tried to explain to him that he must be careful, that sin, like an evil presence lies at the door desiring to rule over him and ruin him. God told Cain that he must rule over it or it would rule over him.

Long nursed sin in a person's heart can pervert his senses. It did this to Cain who finally enticed his brother out into the field, away from others, where with cold heart he murdered his brother.

Since the fall of Adam, we are all in the same position as Cain. Sin, like a roaring lion continually screams at our door desiring to kick it down and eat us alive, but we must control it or it will kill us for eternity. Man, I don't care how righteous you may think you are; we all have the seeds of death within us. Jesus tells us that if we even wish a man dead we have killed him already in our hearts. We are all wicked like mean little children hatching all manner of evil in our hearts and if we will live and not die, we must master it or it will master us.

One watches a teen aged boy with nothing better to do than to sit at a computer and hatch up ideas to put pop ups, viruses, and worms in someone else's computer just for the evil grinning fun of it. He desires to make trouble for others that he cannot even see. Others hack into banks and government computers in order to steal or just make trouble for them and they think it is cute and that they are being "bright". Can't you see them grinning with pride?

Others will shoot a gun into a dwelling, not knowing nor caring who or what they hit. Young men will stand on a street corner and sell narcotics to children never giving it a thought that they are ruining a child's life before he has a life. Grown men will use children, without a flicker of the eye, both girls and boys to calm their sexual burning, never caring that old women in their 70's and 80's still cringe and have nightmares at the rape they suffered as a child. It is said that at the time of a rape, a girl stops growing emotionally. It curdles one's life and it never goes away.

A man or a woman will cheat on their mate and wipe their mouth and say they have done nothing wrong. A woman or a man, even in a church, will pass on a lie about a person in the next pew never considering the hurt and ruination they are causing. We are indeed evil from our baby hood. When was the last time you had to teach a child who can barely talk to lie? It is as natural to them as opening their eyes in the morning. Yes, we definitely have the seeds of death within us.

Although the penalty for murder is death, God, in His mercy did not kill Cain. He did, however, curse him and drive him out from His presence. Cain was a farmer, but from henceforth, the ground would never bear for him again. I once knew a man who desired with all of his heart to be a farmer, but his potatoes, when harvested, were the size of marbles. His corn was infested with worms and his apple trees would not bear. One wonders what this man had done that God so cursed the work of his hands.

Cain would be a wanderer on the earth, not fit company for God or his family ever more. So he took his wife and went out from the presence of the Lord. It is interesting to note that here, again, right from the very beginning, when we sin we go out from the presence of the Lord. It is said that the Bible will keep one from sinning, but sin will keep one from prayer to God and the Bible.

Cain dwelt in the land of Nod (wandering) to the east of the closed off Garden of Eden. It was bad enough that the family could look at Eden, but could not go there, but now Cain could not even fellowship with his family. This is usually another side effect of our sins. It almost always breaks up the family.

As an aside, Adam and Eve had many children, so we can take it that Cain, much like Abraham later, married one of his sisters. There was no law against such a marriage until the time of Moses, some 2500 years later. The gene pool had not yet built up enough recessive genes to cause trouble to one's offspring.

Cain built a city and it was from his line that other murderers began to murder and with the seventh generation from Adam, Lamech indulged in the first polygamous marriage. His first wife's name was Adah, meaning ornament and his second wife was Zillah, meaning seductress. They didn't seem to mind the merger. This should give us some idea of what his wives were all about.

By the time of Lamech, the culture was probably fairly advanced. He had one son, Jabel, who seemed to have a corner on the cattle market. This might indicate that the ungodly line from Adam was probably already eating meat which it was not legal to do until God allowed it after the flood. In the Garden of Eden, the whole earth was given vegetation to eat.

Then there was Jubal, a musician. His name means "undulate". It reminds one of the dance halls of today and tells us about all we need to know about that. Tubal-Cain was a metallurgist, an occupation that was quite lucrative whose secrets were usually kept within a family forcing others to purchase only from them. Lamech himself was a bigamist, a braggart, a murderer, and a blasphemer who appears to spit in God's face with his remarks about God's curse on Cain. Jesus speaks of the wheat and the tares (weeds) and Cain's line represented the weeds and never amounted to much. God soon disposes of any information about that line and gives Adam and Eve another more righteous son to replace Abel, called Seth. Then from the time of Seth's son, Enosh, men from Seth's line, began to call upon the name of the Lord.

From the line of Seth, the Godly line, there came men such as Enoch, who walked with God and he was not, for God took him. Enoch and Elijah were the only two men who were so righteous that God raptured them into heaven alive; and then Noah came along whose name means "rest" and by his time he was the only righteous man left on earth. Then came the flood to destroy all mankind, except Noah and his family, because man had become corrupt (so rotten as to be useless) on the face of the earth. As we look to the story as far as we have progressed, it is not a pretty picture and we see little hope for mankind. But hold on, there is another story.

CHAPTER 11

THE APPOINTMENT

(John 4):

In both John 4, as well as Genesis 4, the results of the fall of Adam and Eve in the Garden can be plainly seen. However, there appears to be somewhat of a difference. One difference we see in Genesis 4, is that man begins to call upon God. In John 4, it is noteworthy that it is God who calls upon mankind (or in this case, womankind).

Also in John 4, man is on the brink of the New Covenant. A covenant is sort of a contract or an agreement that God has made with man. In the Old Testament, before the birth of Christ, God's people were under the old covenant of the law as found in the first five books of the Bible. The people were tied to Temple worship and the animal sacrifice system.

In the New Covenant (contract or agreement given by God) those who believe in Jesus and follow Him, are under grace. Grace is basically an unearned gift from God. In other words, the death of Jesus on the cross takes the place of the temple worship and the sacrificial system for the forgiveness of man's sins. The word Gospel means "good news" and this is indeed good news:

> "For by grace (an unearned or unmerited gift) you have been saved through faith (believing Jesus), and

that not of yourselves; it is the gift of God, 9 not of (your own) works, lest anyone should boast." Eph 2:8-9 NKJV

In John 4, Jesus sees that He must move on. When John the Baptist began baptizing in the Jordan River near Jerusalem, it caused an uproar within the ranks of the Jewish leaders. Now Jesus sees that there is about to be an even worse uproar if He does not leave.

Then we have a curious statement that Jesus "needed" to go through Samaria. There are several problems here. One is going through Samaria. Samaria was a district that divided Israel. It was located midway between Jerusalem in the south and the Sea of Galilee in the north. The Jews did not go through Samaria. In fact, if they wished to go from Jerusalem to the north of Israel near the Sea of Galilee they would leave Jerusalem, cross the Jordan River to the east, go north, then cross back over the Jordan River to the west after they had passed Samaria. A good map would show that they were going miles out of their way just to avoid Samaria.

One must know a quick bit of history to understand this going miles out of their way to get to the Galilee. Because of the politics of King Solomon's son, Rehoboam, about 931 B.C., the ten northern tribes of Israel split away from the two southern tribes making two countries of Israel rather than one.

In time the northern kingdom became so wicked that about 722 B.C., God allowed their enemies, the Assyrians, to overtake them and the Assyrians shipped most of the Israelites out to other countries replacing them with pagan Gentiles from other countries that they had conquered. The northern kingdom then became a mixed multitude, part Israeli and part Gentile. These so called half breeds worshiped in a sort of illegitimate temple worship; not in Jerusalem, the legal place to worship, but they had set up a temple on Mount Gerizim in Samaria.

The Jews hated the Samaritans, refused to speak to them, considered them lowly half breeds, and felt contaminated if they even went through their country. So our first problem is here we have Jesus, a Jew, who puts aside prejudice and heads for Samaria. You see, God does not suffer from the human sickness of prejudice. He loves us all. Like flowers, He thinks we are all beautiful.

Our second problem is why did He "need" to go through Samaria. As we proceed, we see that about noon Jesus comes to a place called Sychar. Being hot and tired he takes a seat by Joseph's well to rest and sends the disciples on into town for provisions.

About this time a woman comes to the well and Jesus asks for a drink. This poses yet other problems. First, the woman is somewhat belligerent as she rudely informs Him that Jews do not speak to Samaritans and second, it was a total breach of etiquette for a man, especially a Jewish man, to speak to a woman, especially a Samaritan woman, in public.

Well, God has been known to break every human rule in the book when He wants to get something done and we suspect that Jesus "needed" to go through Samaria, because He knew He had an appointment with this woman. She didn't know it, but He did. He has an appointment with all of us at one time or another, so don't miss your appointment.

Jesus wanted to tell this woman that He had Spiritual water for her, living water (the Holy Spirit), but the woman, much like Nicodemus, was not living on a spiritual plane. It is interesting that two such different people from such different strata in life should find themselves in the same spiritual condition, that of death. All her mind could grasp was a worldly situation. All she could think about was not having to lug water from that well every day; so she asks Him for this living water. But like every other time God deals with people, He must deal with their sins first. Jesus tells her to go get her husband.

So we have yet another problem and that is, what kind of woman was this who would come to the well at high noon when there were no other women at the well? Good women generally met and gossiped at the well when they went for water either early in the morning or late in the afternoon when it was a bit cooler. This woman came alone in the hottest part of the day. Why? Because she, who had had five husbands, was now living with a man in an unmarried state and was probably the talk of the town. No, so called, decent woman would have anything to do with her.

Again, God has no time for the foolish prejudices of humans. Jesus had said at another time when questioned about the company He kept, that He had not come to call the righteous, but sinners to repentance [31]. Jesus had a wonderful dry sense of humor. What He didn't say at that time was that there are no righteous. All are sinners. He did not, however, bother to explain the joke to the Jewish leaders and they, of course, didn't get it.

Returning to our story, the woman at the well had been found out. When Jesus informed her that He knew all about her five husbands and her present situation, as most unsaved people do, she changed the subject. Now she wants to argue theology. Where should one worship. What church is the real church, what about the heathen, and on it goes. Jesus informs her that salvation is definitely of the Jews (He was the saving Jew); but the day was coming when where one worships will not be the question, but how one worships. In the coming days, people will worship in truth and in their spirit by way of the Holy Spirit. The buildings at both Jerusalem and Garizim would soon become

---

[31] See Matthew 9:13.

unimportant and disappear. It is the heart that matters.

Jesus was giving her the prophecy that it would not be but about thirty some years before there would be no temple standing in which to worship. The Jewish temple would be burned to the ground and torn apart in 70 A.D. by the Romans not to rise again until the seven year Tribulation period which, after some 2,000 years, has not yet arrived.

When the woman tells Jesus that she is expecting the Messiah, she, a Samaritan and a woman, is the first person to whom He speaks plainly as He tells her that He is the Messiah who is to come and has come. It is interesting how women were supposed to be too dumb to matter; yet Jesus included them in and shared some of His deepest secrets with them. He had not yet told the public openly that He was the Messiah.

As the disciples are returning the woman is so flustered that she leaves her water jar and runs to the city to the women —? No, to the men. The women would never have listened to her, but this women knew how to talk to men. Maybe that is why she was chosen. It was to the men of the city she went with the good news that the Messiah, the Christ, Who was to come had now come.

Well, to finish a great story, unlike His own people, the Jews, who would not receive Him, many of the Samaritans believed Him. Not only did they believe Him, and believe that He was the Christ, the

Savior of the world, but they urged Him to stay with them and He stayed there two days. By this act, Jesus drew an extra line of emphasis under the words "whosoever will, may come".

As we finish this chapter, when Jesus finally reached the Galilee a nobleman came to him demanding that Jesus come and heal his son right away. One wonders why Jesus seemed so harsh, when He then complained that the people of Galilee would not receive Him unless they see signs and wonders, until we look back at the Samaritans.

The Samaritans, who weren't even of His own people, the Jews, asked for no miracles, no food, no healings, nothing. All they wanted was Jesus and to hear what He had to say to them. They were so hungry for Him that they didn't just ask Him to stay, they urged Him to stay with them. While on the other hand, as He returned to His own people in the Galilee, by and large they didn't want Him, they wanted miracles. "Come quick and heal my son. Don't do anything else until you do this", etc.

They followed Him because He fed them, healed them, and raised them from the dead. It was a hard nut for Jesus to swallow as He left those hated half breed Samaritans who loved Him, only to encounter His own people, most of whom had little use for him personally. We need to think clearly about this when we listen to the "name it and claim it" preachers of today who merely want, want, want, *from* Jesus. They do not, however, seem to want Jesus.

Of course Jesus healed the child, and that from a distance; which He probably intended to do anyway. However, there must have been something in the demanding voice of the nobleman that spoke to Jesus regarding how thankful the Samaritans were at His coming and how blase' His own people were toward Him. It must have hurt Him terribly.

CHAPTER 12

HELP, I THINK I'M IN THE WRONG CHURCH:

As we wind down this study, the two books we are studying now begin to move apart like a river that splits and goes in two directions. Genesis goes its way showing how God dealt with His people early in the history of the world; and Jesus, in the book of John, goes His way teaching and accomplishing the things He came to do.

The most important decision that everyone must make in this life is, what am I going to do about God and His Son Jesus, the Christ? Shall I receive Jesus as my Lord and Savior and walk with God or shall I just move on and return to my old life with nothing having been accomplished or changed for the better? If you choose to move on, the Bible will make little or no sense to you. However, if you choose the bus to Sheboygan (Heaven), the one Jesus is driving, and get on board, you have a great adventure ahead of you. **Jesus is the sweetheart of Heaven. God the Father speaks of Him and the Holy Spirit never speaks of Himself, but He speaks of the Heaven beloved Son** [32]**, Jesus. God sent prophets to the people of earth, but they only murdered them. Last of all, He has sent His beloved and only begotten Son, Jesus** [33] **to get you.**

---

[32] See John 16:7-15.
[33] See Matthew 21:33-41.

You can get on board the right bus right now by way of prayer. The following prayer is just an example. The important thing is to ask. Jesus tells us that if we ask, we will receive.

> You may pray: Father God, I thank you that Jesus died on the cross that my sins may be forgiven. I ask that my sins be forgiven now. I ask Jesus to be my Lord and Savior. Thank you for forgiving my sins and giving me eternal life. I ask you to come into my life and make me the kind of person you want me to be. I ask all of these things in the name of Jesus. Amen.

If you have prayed this prayer, as a new Christian the next thing you should do is to begin reading the Bible daily and pray that God will help you find a church that teaches the Bible; the church He wants you to attend. Today finding the right church can be a real problem. God has told us that there will come a time when there will be a famine, not of food, but of the word of God. This time seems to be here in that few churches today are teaching the Bible.

What is the main characteristic of a "real" church, the one you should be in? It is love of Jesus and each other and the expository teaching of the word of God, the Bible. If these three things are not present, it is doubtful that you are where God wants you.

What is expository teaching of the Bible? It is teaching (explaining) the Bible, book by book, chapter by chapter. A lot of other things may be put into the mix in a church, some good and some not so good or even rather bad, but no matter what else is put into the mix, the study of the Bible is at the top of the list. If a church teaches the Bible, sooner or later, that church will get it right. If a church does not teach the Bible book by book, chapter by chapter, it is time to move on to another church until you find one that is teaching it; because It is important to know that a Biblically malnourished Christian has no strength to fight Satan and a church that doesn't teach the Bible is nothing more than a social club. In II Timothy 4:2, Paul tells Timothy, pastor of the church at Ephesus, to:

> "Preach the word! Be ready in season and out of season. Convince, rebuke, exhort, with all long suffering and teaching."

Sometimes people do not want to hear the word and it becomes "out of season". What does God say about that? He says teach it anyway.

God doesn't say spend all of your church time pandering to the youth and playing deafening music to draw them into the church. If they loved your children, they wouldn't want to make them deaf; and if kids are just looking for excitement they will soon get bored with church and move on anyway.

He doesn't say teach mini topical sermons, hunt and pecked out of context and beat the sheep to death with them. Today preachers are taught that because people have the attention span of a three minute old bug, they need to get a bunch of gimmicks in their churches and preach nine minute sermons. Not true at all. Remember it is the Devil who is the liar. People can sit in front of a three hour movie with eyes wide open or spend hours sitting in front of a ball game. If the preacher is filled with the Holy Spirit and not lazy he will study and thus make his sermons interesting and the people will listen.

God didn't say beat the sheep; He said "feed my sheep" with the word of God, the whole Gospel. God also didn't say preach on money for weeks on end. This is either greed or the pastor is in over his head financially. Maybe God doesn't want him to have that bigger and more fancy church. What God did say is **read the word and explain the sense of it.** If the Pastor does this he will ultimately reach every subject that God cares about, even money. That is what expository teaching of the Bible is all about.

However, beware of churches that teach some other book instead of the Bible or put some other book ahead of the Bible. Remember the first chapter of this study? "The itinerary (the Bible) is always right". Even Sunday School classes get off the track by teaching so called "how to" or "experience" books without knowing what God has had to say about a certain subject. Believe me, experiences differ. Always go to the Bible first. Whatever disagrees with the Bible should be discarded.

There is, however, a difference between "how to" or "experience" books and commentaries. Commentaries, are merely teaching comments by one teacher or another about a passage of Scripture. Commentaries take a book of the Bible and explain it chapter by chapter. Some are good and some not so good. It must be remembered, though, that these are written by men, not God. Only the Bible is God's word, but many commentary writers are very good teachers and can open up understanding of the Bible for those who have recently come to read it. A good thing a Bible reader can do is read a chapter of the Bible and then take a look at a good commentary about that chapter.

There are all kinds of commentaries. A good one volume Commentary to begin with is *"THE WYCLIFFE BIBLE COMMENTARY"* [34]. This is a commentary put out by the people who go all over the world translating the Bible into different languages.

A second good commentary is a two volume set, one for the Old Testament and one for the New Testament, *"THE BIBLE KNOWLEDGE COMMENTARY"*. This commentary is an expository

---

[34] All of the following recommended books will be listed in the Bibliography under their appropriate headings.

teaching of the Bible by the Faculty of Dallas Theological Seminary. Don't be put off by the fact that it is written by faculty members. This commentary is simply written and carefully written and is quite good. It has a bit more information than the first commentary mentioned, but they run in the same line.

Then if you want to read devotional commentaries say on a certain book of the Bible, there are many. However, some favorites are *"EXPLORING THE GOSPELS: JOHN"* and *"EXPLORING GENESIS"*, both by John Phillips. These are very good to finish out the two books we are studying in this small study. Other good commentaries on the book of John are *"THE GOSPEL ACCORDING TO JOHN"* by G. Campbell Morgan and *"ADDRESSES ON THE GOSPEL OF JOHN"* by H.A. Ironside. Another one volume commentary on one book is *"GENESIS; a devotional commentary"* by W. H. Griffith Thomas. There may be a problem locating this one in that it may be out of print. However, some book stores, such as Borders, can find out of print books and can get it for you. It can touch one's heart and is well worth looking for.

There are also "many volume" commentaries that can be had. They are, however, rather expensive to get the whole set. Many can be purchased one book at a time. A good beginning set that can be purchased is a set written by J. Vernon McGee, the radio Bible teacher. It is called *"THRU THE BIBLE COMMENTARY SERIES"*. He takes one book of the Bible at a time and writes comments on it explaining the pertinent points of each chapter.

There are many good studies on the Bible that can be purchased or ordered at any good Bible book store. If such is not available to you, you can always look up Christian book stores on the internet. However, this can be tricky in that many book stores carry books that pan the Bible rather than studying the Bible. It is always good to pray about it, because God will show you if you are getting into apostate (incorrect) teaching.

The important thing to remember is that in these last days it is imperative to study the Bible for yourself in that many churches have given up on the Bible or are teaching strange doctrines and "feel good" sermons. Remember, God tells us that if we don't know what He has told us, we are open to believing any lie that the Devil whispers in our ears.

We have left for last the matter of Love. First, God loves us. He cares what happens to us and if our life is in a mess or our heart is full of sorrow, He wants to and is able to do something about it. Jesus tells us that NOTHING is impossible with God. God has a plan for us and He means it for our good. By the same token, He tells us that we need to love our Christian brother or sister (other Christians), and that goes for Pastors loving their congregations, too. We also must love our Pastor enough to pray for him, especially that he will teach in the power of the Holy Spirit.

First we need to know what love is. Love is a choice. It is not necessarily that warm fuzzy feeling we get about someone we are fond of. To find out what God has to say about love, we turn to I Corinthians 13.

> "Though I speak with the tongues of men and of angels, but have not love, I have become sounding brass or a clanging cymbal ... Love suffers long and is kind; love does not envy; love does not parade itself, is not puffed up (arrogant); does not rejoice in iniquity, but rejoices in the truth; bears all things, believes all things, hopes all things, endures all things. Love never fails. But whether there are prophecies, they will fail; whether there are tongues, they will cease; whether there is knowledge, it will vanish away ... And now abide faith, hope, love, these three; but the greatest of these is love.

Never fear, this takes a lifetime. Some of us are still working on the "kindness" part. How do we know that we are in a loving church? It will take a while to find this out in any church, but after you have been in a church for awhile and are trying to decide whether or not to join that particular church, a good thing to ask yourself is:

"If I were being hunted down by the Government merely because I am a Christian, is there anyone in this church whom I would trust enough to take me in and not turn me in?"

If the answer to this question is no, it might be better to start praying about moving on to another church, because, you need help, beloved, you may be in the wrong church.

SUGGESTED READINGS ON APOLOGETICS

(SEE CHAPTER 3:)

Norman Geisler (1996) *"WHEN SKEPTICS ASK"*, Baker Books, Grand Rapids, MI,;

Josh McDowell (1993), *"EVIDENCE THAT DEMANDS A VERDICT"*, Thomas Nelson Publishers, Nashville, Tenn.,

D. James Kennedy (1997), *"SKEPTICS ANSWERED"*, Multnomah Books, Sisters Ore.

SUGGESTED READING ON CREATION VS. EVOLUTION

Paul Copan and William Lane Craig, *"CREATION OUT OF NOTHING"*, Baker Academic, Grand Rapids, MI, 2004.

Michael J. Behe, *"DARWIN'S BLACK BOX"*, The Free Press, New York, N.Y., 2003.

Duncan, Hall, Ross, Archer, Irons, Kline, edited by David G. Hagopian, *"THE GENESIS DEBATE"*, Crux Press, Inc., Mission Viejo, CA, 2001.

Edited by Carl Wieland, (written by 22 Scientists), *"THE GENESIS FILES"*, Master Books, Green Forest, AR, 2004.

Edited by John F. Ashton, PhD, (written by 50 Scientists), *"IN SIX DAYS"*, Master Books, Green Forest, AR, 2002.

Walter Brown, PhD, *"IN THE BEGINNING, COMPELLING EVIDENCE FOR CREATION AND THE FLOOD"* Center for Scientific Creation, Phoenix, AZ, 2001.

D. Russell Humphreys, Ph.D., *"STARLIGHT AND TIME: SOLVING THE PUZZLE OF DISTANT STARLIGHT IN A YOUNG UNIVERSE"*, Master Books, Green Forest, AZ, 1994.

James Perloff, *"TORNADO IN A JUNKYARD, THE RELENTLESS MYTH OF DARWINISM"* , Refuge Books, Arlington, MA, 1999.

BIBLIOGRAPHY

All Scripture References:

The Bible, *"THE NEW KING JAMES VERSION"*, Thomas Nelson, Inc. 1982

James Perloff, *"TORNADO IN A JUNKYARD; The Relentless Myth of Darwinism"*, Refuge Books, Arlington, MA, 1999.

ONE OR TWO VOLUME COMMENTARIES ON THE WHOLE BIBLE:

John F. Walvoord and Roy B. Zuck, *"THE BIBLE KNOWLEDGE COMMENTARY; An Exposition of the Scriptures by Dallas Seminary Faculty: Old Testament edition"*, Victor Books, 1985.

John F. Walvoord and Roy B. Zuck, *"THE BIBLE KNOWLEDGE COMMENTARY; an exposition of the scriptures by Dallas Seminary faculty: New Testament edition"*, Victor Books, 1983.

Edited by Charles F. Pfeiffer and Everett F. Harrison, *"THE WYCLIFFE BIBLE COMMENTARY"*, Moody Press, Chicago, Ill., 1962 & 1990.

DEVOTIONAL COMMENTARIES ON INDIVIDUAL BIBLE BOOKS IN ONE VOLUME:

Genesis:
John Phillips, *"EXPLORING GENESIS"*, Moody Press, Chicago, Ill, 1980.

W. H. Griffith Thomas, D.D., *"GENESIS, A DEVOTIONAL COMMENTARY"*, Wm. B. Eerdmans publishing co., Grand Rapids, Mich.,1953.

John:
H.A. Ironside, Litt. D., *"ADDRESSES ON THE GOSPEL OF JOHN"*, Loizeaux Brothers, Inc., Neptune, New Jersey, 1978.

John Phillips, *"EXPLORING THE GOSPELS: JOHN"*, Loizeaux Brothers, Neptune, New Jersey, 1988.

G. Campbell Morgan, *THE GOSPEL ACCORDING TO JOHN"*, Fleming H. Revell Co., Old Tappan, New Jersey, undated.

Dr. Brashear received a Bachelor of Arts in Theological Studies; a Master of Arts in Theological Studies; and a Doctorate of Ministry in Theological Studies from Vision International College & University, Ramona, CA.

She previously spent 30 years as a Court Reporter in the following court settings: Los Angeles County Superior Court System; Department of Justice, Immigration and Naturalization Svc., Deportation Hearings; in the Federal Court System; and with various private reporting firms.

Dr. Brashear has been engaged in reading and class work studies of the Bible for approximately forty years and has taught Bible in the California Prison System and in several prison aftercare homes. She has also taught independent studies with police and court personnel.

www.ingramcontent.com/pod-product-compliance
Lightning Source LLC
LaVergne TN
LVHW011421080426
835512LV00005B/200